A
Hawaiian Lū'au
with Sam Choy
and the Mākaha Sons

For all of Hawaiian heart and
Hawaiian ancestry living both in
Hawai'i and outside of Hawai'i
who perpetuate the kūpuna
traditions of lū'au and mele.

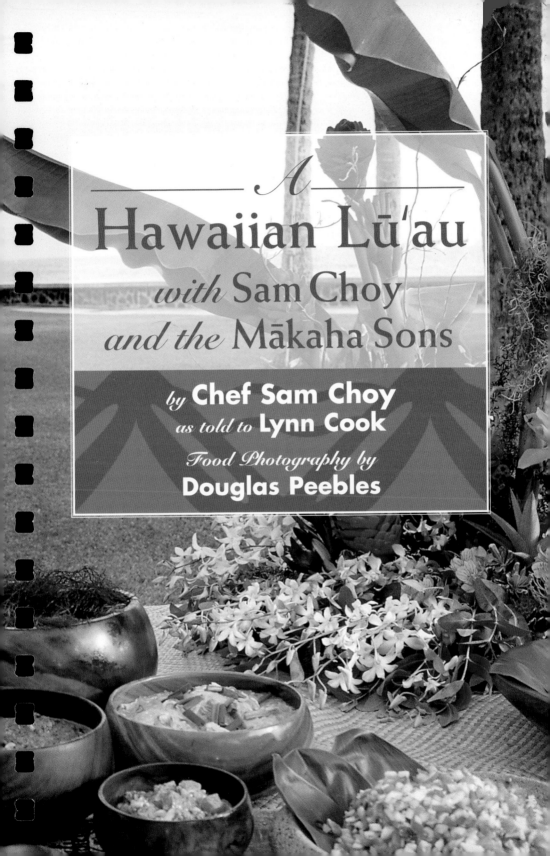

A Hawaiian Lū'au

with Sam Choy
and the Mākaha Sons

by **Chef Sam Choy**
as told to **Lynn Cook**

Food Photography by
Douglas Peebles

Library of Congress Catalog Card Number: 2002111533

First Printing, November 2003
1 2 3 4 5 6 7 8 9

All photos by Douglas Peebles unless otherwise noted.

Cover design by Jane Hopkins
Book design by Mardee Domingo Melton

ISBN 1-56647-573-2

Sam Choy: www.samchoy.com
The Mākaha Sons: www.makahasons.com

Mutual Publishing, LLC
1215 Center Street, Suite 210
Honolulu, Hawai'i 96816
Ph: (808) 732-1709
Fax: (808) 734-4094
e-mail: mutual@mutualpublishing.com
www.mutualpublishing.com
Printed in Korea

Introduction

Sam Choy and the Mākaha Sons are the perfect combination to serve up a Hawaiian Lū'au. Both are household words in Hawai'i, both are unofficial good will ambassadors bringing Hawai'i to all parts of the globe. Both are Hawaiian, both are leaders in their field. And together they provide the key ingredients to a successful lū'au—lū'au and song.

Friends for over ten years, the Mākaha Sons appear regularly on Sam's TV show, Sam Choy's Kitchen. They say they are learning to cook although Sam says they are learning to eat. On the other hand, Sam makes the occasional musical accompaniment usually during rehearsal.

They work well together. With Sam blending the flavors and The Sons the harmony together making beautiful music.

This corroboration provides the best of the food and music for the lū'au occasion. Just add the guests, the warmth, stir well and have fun.

Table of Contents

PART ONE
Talk Story

"*T*here were around thirty people at the lū'au at first. George and a cousin…dug a pit and roasted a small pig wrapped in chicken wire in it for a day and a half before Christmas…. Dennis was impressed by the gathering—the people did seem all of one family, huge men who shook his hand with their large, soft hands, huge women in muumuus who sat around in the shade fanning themselves and talking story with the aroma of pork escaped from the ground, and they all talked with the familiarity of a family even though, as he understood, they hadn't seen one another in a year."

"… *T*he cars parked in front of the Maunawili house went right out of sight in both directions, ... and both the front and back porches had an absurd profusion of slippers, shoes and high heels piled up by those who went into the house. One Waianae cousin came in a suit with a vest and gold watch chain, and Kenika found him sitting in the grass taking off his shoes before going into the house, and told the man that he really didn't have to do that, but he said, nah nah, s'okay. His hand was shaken by the meaty hands of dozens of uncles and cousins and friends, and he was mauled by huge women wearing startlingly bright muumuus, who planted kisses on his cheeks and put leis over his head until they rose all the way to his nose. ...

A three-man guitar and ukulele band showed up just after noon, and played Hawaiian songs as the people chattered. George and his friends drew the chicken wire-wrapped pig out of the pit in the backyard at two, but Kenika thought it surely had to be superfluous because there was so much food everywhere, heaps of little crabs, shrimp, various kinds of fish and octopus chunks, Japanese and Chinese and Filipino delicacies, little squares of coconut cake, beer, juice for the kids. But with the pig came the sweet potato, poi, lomi salmon, fried chicken, and more obscure vegetables and meats and desserts from the aunties and uncles and calabash cousins of different backgrounds and mixes of races. ..."

– *The Red Wind* by Ian MacMillan

A Hawaiian Lū'au *with Sam Choy and the Mākaha Sons*   **2**

"When the sand was dug away from the imu and they cut away the canvas, smoke wooshed through the night carrying the sweet roasting scent of meat. The banana leaves and ti leaves were scorched black and the skins of the pigs were steamed a crispy sizzling brown. Each pig was hoisted on the a papapuaa, a huge koa wood platter...

The table was covered with tapa cloth and layers of fern and ti leaves. Jacaranda and shell ginger vines laced about the table. Floral displays of orchid and plumeria sprays wound about bird-of-paradise were spaced at intervals along the table. At each setting was a red hibiscus, the official flower of Hawaii.

The center of the table was piled with fruit: tender, milk-filled coconuts, sweet-meated papayas, avocados from Hana Maui, malala peels of raw sugar cane, slices of watermelon, Isabella grapes bunched in high grassy clusters, mangoes, alligator pears, juicy rose-colored guavas, wild bananas and halakahiki—standing pineapples which appeared whole and uncut but which had been hollowed, corded and cut into long spears and reassembled with the top as a lid. Long slivers of wood had been stuck into the tops of the pineapples, and on these were the pupu—Hawaiian hors d'oeuvres—including succulent pieces of marinated Tera-yaki steak, raw mullet cut in tempting cubes and dusted with paakai salt, chunks of tiny parboiled lobsters fresh out of Kalama Bay, small alemihi crabs with their shells pierced so that the sweet meat could be filled with coconut pudding.

While the men quartered and sliced the three pigs, the young girls brought to the table big calabash bowls of jumbo shrimp, sushi, and saimin, and relish bowls of ake raw liver mixed with chili peppers, kukui nuts crushed and baked with paakai salt, and limu, strips of dried kelp and opihi seaweed. On koa wood platters the girls brought marinated slices of moray eel, and pinkish tidbits of barbecued squid tentacles, and stewed fern stalks served hot and covered with a melted butter and honey sauce and tasting something like asparagus. Coconut half shells filled with Chinese crackseed and roasted macadamia nuts supplanted the pupu. For liquid refreshment there was pineapple juice, chilled and poured into hollowed husks, guava juice, coconut milk straight from the shell, and beer, whisky, okolehao,

Talk Story

and Mai Tai, a heady mixture of rums sipped with straws from pineapple husks.

As the pupu was being devoured, the girls brought in platters of lomilomi—fresh raw king salmon mixed with chopped onions and tomatoes and minced with the fingers; moa—tender white meat of chicken mixed with the Hawaiian spinach called taro roots and coconut cream and served in coconut half shells; boned chicken baked in coconut shells with wild rice and pineapple and served in koa wood calabashes floated with mint-flavored spun sugar; breadfruit roasted over kiawe coals so a crust formed about the succulent inner meat; thick rare slices of pipioma roast beef; heikaukau rock crab with tartar sauce sprinkled with paakai salt, and the all-inclusive welakaukau Hawaiian hot stew.

There was fried butterfish with garlic sauce, i-a paakai salt fish, uahi smoked fish, maloo dried fish slabs of the wonderfully fresh ahi tuna, boneless chuck of ono which is something like swordfish but tastier, kawelea fish, barracuda, barbecued black sea bass, and finally, as it was taken from the imu and the scorched leaves unwrapped from it, the sizzling limu-white mahimahi dolphin, the most glorious-tasting fish in the sea.

It took six men to carry the three platters of puaa pigs to the table, the meat still steaming, the pink-scrubbed skin turned a crispy brown, the platters surrounded by the yams and wild bananas that had been cooked with the meat for the last five hours in the underground oven.

At every place there was a large goblet carved from a coconut shell that had been thinned and polished and scalloped around the brim, and in the goblet was a quart of that most mystifying of food, the mainstay of the Hawaiian luau—poi."

– *Diamond Head* by Peter Gilman

"The mat, almost hidden under fresh leaves, ferns, and flowers, was laden with fruits and vegetables of every kind the lands of O'ahu could offer. From far and near they were gathered in: coconuts, sugarcane, pineapples, oranges, watermelons, guavas, bananas, mangoes, bowls full of red prickly pears of the cactus plant, freed of their spiny skins and bathed in their blood-colored juices; pyramids of baked taro, sweet potatoes, white potatoes, and breadfruits, of raw cabbages, love apples, onions both green and round, chili peppers, radishes, alligator pears, and wooden bowls holding a dozen different kind of seaweeds.... Already awaiting each of us were a huge calabash full of poi; platters of dried beef, dried fish, and dried squid; a coconut-shell cup holding crystals of red salt; another full of that delectable relish prepared by mixing fragments of baked kukui nutmeats with rock salt and crisp red seaweed; a silver fingerbowl with yellow 'ilima flowers floating upon the water; a nest of sparkling glasses to hold any drink we might choose. ...

Now, coming before us almost on their knees, a long line of servers brought in bowls and trenchers of hot meats, still steaming from the earth-ovens in which they had been cooked: tender flesh of pig, dog, beef, veal, mutton, and lamb, rich with gobbets of fat and flakes of crusted skin; convoys of whole chickens, pigeons, and plovers arranged around native ducks and geese. Then came the provender of the sea: raw or cooked, baked or steamed, whole or broken, they were more numerous than were the meats and fowls: mullet, 'opelu, kawakawa, aholehole, 'opakapaka, 'a'awa, ulua, and papio, several kinds of tunas, mahimahi, eels, squid, crabs, lobsters, 'opihi, pipipi, wana, sea cucumbers, even that new and costly delicacy, salted salmon imported from Oregon. Never in my whole life had my nose been treated to so many enticing aromas, my stomach to so many assaults upon its strength."

– *Ka'a'awa* by O.A. Bushnell

Talk Story

The Mākaha Sons

When we were kids, a family lūʻau was never a single-day affair. The evening's food and festivities always flowed into a mini-lūʻau the next day, a breakfast or brunch for the out-of-towners and the diehards who stayed around to help clean-up. It was understood that part of their job was to work at polishing off the leftover food, which was always plentiful.

Hawaiʻi has never seen a lūʻau where there was too little food. Lūʻau always seem to start out small and grow until they are huge, not only in the number of guests but the variety of delicious dishes. With our big families in Hawaiʻi, the invitation list never seems to stop growing, because you always want to make sure that absolutely no one in the islands is offended! And of course the invited guests usually show up with their own friends in tow.

In the old days, back when people mostly worked just one job—or maybe didn't go to work at all—there were lots of helping hands to prepare the lūʻau. Aunty could make the laulau. Uncle would hunt the pig. And cousins would pitch in to dig the imu. Today, the demands of work and modern life have introduced a lot more catered dishes to our lūʻau. But there are people who still live in the old style and can put on a lūʻau in the traditional way that we loved so well.

One lūʻau treat that hasn't changed over the years is the chance to be around our aunties and uncles, kids, cousins, and most especially our kapuna, our treasured elders who share stories of the way life used to be. As boys, we would sit and listen to their lessons and memories that seemed almost magical to us. We've never grown tired of hearing those stories.

And, of course, lūʻau are all about music, second only to the food. As children we would join in the impromptu singing and entertaining—anybody who felt the urge could grab the spotlight. There were always instruments around, ukuleles, harmonicas, guitars, and plenty of people to play them. These days we're never sure if we are invited to lūʻau because someone wants our company, or just because we've become professional musicians! They tell us to come and relax but soon we're asked to play one for Grandma. Then Uncle's favorite…. Even though the older songs are no longer as well known, we enjoy performing them.

For this book, we have compiled some lūʻau favorites—songs that are among our most popular requests when we attend lūʻau—along with the ones we just like to play.

Sam Choy

One of my best memories from childhood is the family gathering, crowded with friends, and tables so full of food that they looked like they would break. I can close my eyes and taste the kālua pig, the squid lū'au, the poi. I can smell the fragrance bouquet from the mix of food that meant just one thing—a lū'au.

In Hawai'i the lū'au is the traditional way of celebrating a special occasion. A wedding, an anniversary, a first birthday, a graduation—whatever the event, Hawaiians jump at the chance to celebrate it with serious eating. No light picnics here. Nor is there anything intimate about it. A lū'au can host as many as five hundred—even five thousand—guests. On the other hand, a lū'au can be much smaller, and held for no reason at all, just a group of family and friends pooling their energy and effort to have fun.

So if you are new to the islands and you find the very concept of a lū'au intimidating, just relax and think of it as a big backyard party. The recipe is simple. You add food, music, maybe some dance, and stir.

When I was growing up, my dad catered a Saturday lū'au on the North Shore of O'ahu. He usually followed the traditional menu, with kālua pig, poi and all the fixings.

My role was to keep from falling into the giant vat while I stirred the syrup, water and pineapple juice for the punch, and to mix the poi without wearing it in on my face, hair and clothes.

Since those days, the lūʻau has grown to include mouth-watering dishes from all the major ethnic groups in the islands—Chinese, Japanese, Filipino and Korean. Today there are no limits to the lūʻau table. If an Australian marries into the family, you'll find shrimp on the barbecue. If your guests are into gourmet trends, or health-conscious eating, the table might feature seared ʻahi and poke in Pacific Rim-cuisine style, fruit and vegetable platters, and maybe some oven-roasted turkey instead of the traditional pig.

In this book I have gathered up all my family favorites, along with some very traditional lūʻau recipes. Then I folded in some "melting pot" recipes and what I call "backyard lūʻau" food, and added in all the "aunties'" favorites. The result may be your best party ever!

Here you'll find Papa's Lūʻau Feast: Traditional Lomilomi Salmon, No-Imu Kālua Pig, My Mom's Squid Lūʻau, da Kine Poke Supreme, Poi, Chicken

Long Rice, Sweet Potato Casserole, and Pineapple Haupia—a truly scrumptious menu. But you also can create a dozen different lū'au menus from other recipes in this book. There are no real rules on mixing and matching. Just make sure your menu isn't heavy with dishes that must be prepared at the last minute. And don't forget to write down every detail. Some family member is sure to say "Hana Hou," do it again! And you'll be ready.

My friends the Mākaha Sons join me in presenting this lū'au cookbook. Moon, John and Jerome have been making people happy with their music for many years, and have played every kind of lū'au party there is. They make my TV show, Sam Choy's Kitchen so much fun it's hard to concentrate on making the food!

It's this island lū'au that I hope you all experience—a happy group of people, coming together to eat and celebrate.

Talk Story: *Sam Choy*

The History of the Lūau

In ancient times lūʻau could last for days. Each type of lūʻau had strict rules dictating what could be eaten and by whom. As soon as it was certain that a young woman was to have her first child, the father began raising a pig for the ʻAhaʻaina Mawaewae feast that was celebrated within twenty-four hours after the child was born. Mullet and taro leaf were required, along with shrimp, seaweed and crab; each being instrumental in the health and well-being of the child. These elaborate preparations would be the last thing a brand new mom today would want to do. And not too many dads can raise a pig on the lānai!

The next really big event was the ʻAhaʻaina Palala; what we now call the first-birthday baby lūʻau. This had strict ceremonial rules and ceremonial foods as well. If the baby was the first-born of the ruling chief, gifts of great value were stored away for the child. Feasting and dance honored the baby. Chants or haku mele, honoring the name of the child, were composed with great diligence in the belief that they might influence the life of the child. Some of these beautiful mele, or songs, are still sung today, combined with hula that has been handed down across the generations.

In earlier times, Queen Liliʻuokalani hosted elegant lūʻau parties for visiting European royalty. And history books recount the 19th-century visit of writer

Robert Louis Stevenson who was entertained by King David Kalākaua and was honored at a lūʻau for seven hundred people. Imu-roasted pig, steamed laulau, poi, fish, sweet potato, seaweed, and coconut were the lūʻau staples then.

By the late 1700s, however, the lūʻau menu had already begun to change from just traditional dishes. The missionaries are credited with the addition of cake. The whalers brought in salted fish that we now call lomilomi salmon. The Chinese gave us chicken long rice. White rice and sushi came from the Japanese. Over the years, the lūʻau has continued to change, mirroring the melting pot of cultures that flavor modern Hawaiʻi.

Hawaiʻi State Archives

Talk Story: *The History of the Lūʻau*

Photo: Alonzo Gartley, Bishop Museum

The Traditional Lūʻau Feast

The lūʻau is a feast that not only celebrates important events, but also cements the bonds of friendship and family. A lūʻau can last the entire weekend, with people arriving on Friday afternoon to begin the preparation. Aunties from the Big Island bring orchids and anthuriums for decoration, along with extended family and friends who pitch in with the preparations, and also launch the pre-lūʻau partying.

By early morning on the day of the big event, it's time to dig the imu, or lūʻau pit and fill it with hot rocks and ti leaves. A pig, often wrapped in chicken wire to hold it together, is lowered into the pit. Other foods—turkeys, laulau (ti leaf bundles of meat and

Eric Futran, *Great Chefs® of Hawaiʻi*

The perfect *imu*, or baking pit, is dug into the earth and lined with volcanic rocks or other rocks that will not split when heated to a high temperature, such as granite (slate, shale, and other sedimentary rocks won't work). A fire is built over the rocks and allowed to burn down until the rocks themselves are extremely hot. The rocks are then spread on the bottom of the pit and pulled to the sides; after the food is added the rocks will be piled on top of the food and the pit covered for slow cooking. The process is similar to that used for a New England clambake.

fish), sweet potatoes, fish—are added. Then everything is covered with leaves, burlap, and soil, and left to steam all day.

'Opihi and limu will have been gathered from the seaside, or purchased at great expense in a local market.

Now the preparation of the other food begins. The day proceeds with a lot of chopping, stirring, and laughter. The side dishes, such as poke, squid lū'au (squid cooked with taro tops and coconut milk), lomilomi salmon (a salad of salted salmon, tomatoes, onions and chili peppers), chicken long rice (a Chinese dish of chicken and bean thread noodles), and haupia or kulolo (coconut or taro puddings) are made ahead.

And there is always poi. Originally poi was made by peeling, cooking, and pounding taro roots into a paste. Today poi is purchased from regional factories, and the product is superior for its smoothness

and consistency. This healthy staple starch is the basis of the traditional Hawaiian diet.

The younger family members decorate the tables and the hall. Long picnic tables may be covered with rolls of paper. Family members and friends then decorate with ti leaves, laua'e ferns, and flowers down the center. A fancier lū'au might have tapa or pareau-designed fabric tablecloths.

Just before the lū'au begins, flavored soda water in bottles, a square piece of coconut cake, red alae salt (coarse sea salt mixed with clay), raw onions, and other condiments are placed at each seat.

The guests arrive in their finest mu'umu'u and aloha shirts. Children are always included and show up scrubbed clean and wearing their best jeans or shorts.

The music strikes up as the guests arrive—either the "cha-lang a-lang" variety that has been played by backyard bands for as long as anyone can remember, or music from a sound system. The hula dancers are the granddaughters, cousins, mothers, or uncles of the people in the group. They may forget some of the movements, but they know the meaning of the dance. It is a gift to their family—their 'ohana.

The party often continues on Sunday. The kālua pig is reheated on top of the stove with cabbage and onions. Other leftovers are heated up and laid out, or left on the stove for people to help themselves.

By early afternoon, everyone is headed home, to the other side of the island, or off to the airport to catch a late plane to a neighbor island. Now the lū'au-givers can collapse—and gather up their memories.

If you give a lū'au yourself, remember that the food should be fresh and plentiful, the preparation shared, and the spirit open and loving.

The Pig and The Imu

The imu, a Hawaiian underground oven, takes work. Planning, digging, preparation and the final product make the imu a total bonding experience. But if it's too much for you, there are caterers who specialize in imu cooking and can do it for you or at least give you some expert advice. Before you get to the imu, however, you'll have to decide the size of your pig, as that will determine how deep you dig your imu.

If your cousin doesn't raise pigs, you can order one from a meat market, a rancher or a slaughterhouse which can de-hair the pig. The pig should be cooked with the skin on to drive the juices deep into the meat while it is cooking.

Eric Futran, *Great Chefs' of Hawai'i*

For the size, about one half pound per person of dressed weight is a good rule of thumb. The pig will lose between thirty and thirty-five percent of weight in the

Eric Futran, *Great Chefs® of Hawai'i*

dressing process. A hundred-pound pig would dress out to sixty-five or seventy pounds, serving 120 persons.

Once you've purchased the pig, you're ready to turn to the imu project. Gather your materials. You'll need kindling wood, koa or other hard wood, rocks, chicken wire, banana leaves or a substitute like green corn husks, burlap, canvas and sand.

Next step? Dig! A pit about two to three feet deep is standard, depending on the size of your pig. If you choose an imu site that has been used before, be sure to empty out all the litter and previously used rocks.

Kindling can be a cardboard box and a splintered two-by-four. Fire it up and add the bigger pieces of wood, then the rocks.

Talk Story: *The Pig and The Imu*

Rocks must be dry. If they are wet, the water inside can expand and explode, sending dangerous shards everywhere. Use round rocks without sharp corners. If you don't have lava rock, use river rock.

While the fire is heating the rocks, cut the banana stocks in two-foot lengths. Make sure they are moist.

A heavy canvas tarp, soaking wet, will help steam the pig. Make sure it is clean and large enough to cover the entire pit.

Once the rocks are white-hot, begin to remove the logs. If you leave pieces of burning wood, the flames can burn the pig.

With the wood removed, thee rocks should be arranged into the shape of the pig's silhouette in the pit.

Completely cover the rocks with banana stock. If you don't have access to banana stock, you can substitute corn stocks, swamp cabbage or cattails.

Gary Hofheimer

A Hawaiian Lūʻau *with Sam Choy and the Mākaha Sons* **22**

Time to carry the pig to the pit. Gill slits by the head end of the pig make it easier. Grab the legs on the other end. Lay it on the spread-out chicken wire. Use tongs to place hot rocks in the shoulder/leg area and in the cavity. Tap rocks to knock off the ash before they go into the pig. Make sure rocks have no corners that can break off or cut into the pig.

Be sure you count the rocks so that when you empty the pig you take out the same number you put in. Then tie up the chicken wire and lift the pig onto the banana-covered hot rocks.

Cover the pig with more banana leaves, longways and crossways, and cover with the wet canvas tarps. Cover the entire area, at least six to twelve inches around the pit onto flat ground. Last, cover the entire mound with six inches of sand. A 125-pound pig takes at least nine hours to cook. You really can't overcook a pig in an imu.

When the time is up, scrape off the sand. Take the canvas tarps off carefully. Don't let any sand fall into the meat. Watch out when you peel back the banana leaves—they are filled with burning steam. Count those rocks again as you remove them.

Open the chicken wire and lift the pig off the fire. Make sure you have plenty of help for this part. Now, take a deep breath and inhale the wonderful fragrance of that pig! Put the pig on a carrier and head for the preparation and serving area. Since the pig is so hot, you'll need to be very careful as you pull it apart. Keep bowls of ice water close for hands that get too hot. The meat should be falling off the bone.

Make sure you leave an adult in charge of the imu area once the pig is removed. Kids love to run and

Talk Story: *The Pig and The Imu*

play at a lūʻau and you don't want imu-ed toes! Pull all wood away from the stones. Lay tarps out to dry away from the party area. Don't leave the site until you are sure that the pit area is safe, cool and that there are no smoldering logs.

A pig can also be cooked in a barbecue pit or in a temporary above-ground outdoor oven built of bricks and lined with sand. The result may not be exactly the same but if the steam and juices are sealed in the pig, it can run a close second to imu-cooked meat.

All the other lūʻau dishes should be ready to serve once the pig is done. My best tip is to place the platter of kālua pig at the end of the buffet line. Let your guests fill their plates with all the other delicious dishes first, and you will have plenty of pig for seconds. Big stainless steel trays are best for holding the pig. Tongs work well for serving. Make sure you have food covers or foil to keep the bugs away. Line up everything on the table ahead of the pig. Now, dig in!

Eric Futran, *Great Chefs' of Hawaiʻi*

Location, Guests and How Can They Help?

*T*here are three things you need to decide. How many people are invited? Where will the party be? And how big is the pig? If you live in the country and have lots of space, the backyard is perfect for a traditional lūʻau with pig roasted in the ground. If you rent your home, don't forget to ask the landlord if digging a big hole in his yard is OK.

If you live in a condo, you'll have to find a lūʻau location to fit the size and shape of the party. A rented hall or a public park is great for a pot luck lūʻau with oven-baked kālua pig. A backyard lūʻau can be great fun, even if you can't do the imu yourself. Best of all is the full-on family lūʻau with an imu, the underground oven.

Your choice of location is determined by how many people are coming to your lūʻau. The time of day is dictated by the length of time it takes to cook the pit in the imu. If you opt for oven-roasted or catered pig, you can open the buffet line almost any time. Just remember the rule, "At a lūʻau we don't ʻeat 'till we are full—we eat 'till we're tired!" Allow time for visiting, singing, dancing and relaxing after dessert. Of course, always add an extra half hour at the end, just for the honihoni (kissing everyone goodbye).

If you are planning on more than one hundred people, form a committee and divide up the tasks. You can make the invitations part of the fun by gathering the family and making your own. Get some bright-colored cards and envelopes, a stamp pad and a tropical flower stamp. The when, where and why part is easy to print on a home computer. Your invitation should read "Aloha Attire." That means comfortable! Pareau for ladies, aloha shirts for the men.

The event you are celebrating can set the theme. There is really no traditional lū'au decor. Lū'au and feast photos from the days of King Kalākaua show the tables long and low, set close to the ground, with everyone sitting on mats. It looks great in pictures, but many of us today would have a hard time getting up once we got down that low.

A tent is nice for sun or rain. Long tables are still the best for the food, and a covering of white butcher paper can thrown away later rather than laundered.

Lū'au decorations don't have to be fancy to be fun. For a simple centerpiece, run a row of tī leaves, or fern or coconut fronds down the center of the table. Then add bouquets of flowers or just scatter handfuls of yellow plumeria blossoms and Vanda orchids. Make sure there are toothpicks for the folks who want to put a flower behind their ear. If flowers aren't available, use fresh fruit mixed in the fern. Later, the kids can eat the centerpiece. You don't need much on the table because it will soon be filled with plates of food. Remember bottles of low-salt soy sauce and little dishes of Hawaiian salt.

Tiki torches are great for the "lū'au look," but nighttime events may need more light. If the power source is convenient, get out the Christmas twinkle lights and string them along the tent or wrap them around the nearby coconut tree. For good light with a glow, try a drop socket (plug-in cord with a light bulb socket at the end) hung inside a Chinese lantern. For bugs, add in a bunch of citronella candles, but keep them away from the food table. The scent is strong.

When it comes to live greenery, find out who has potted palms or a garden full of ginger blossoms. Big buckets filled with rocks will hold tall cut ginger, bamboo, banana leaves, monstera leaves, or bird of paradise stalks. Wrap the bottom in coconut fiber, tapa wrapping paper or tī leaves and tie on a big raffia bow. If tropical foliage isn't available, just about any big potted plant can be wrapped in tapa paper for an island look. No tropical plants around? A bunch of bamboo poles from the garden store with some greens and flowers can help your ambience. Put them in a big bucket, duct tape a plastic bottle midway up, fill it with water and any kind of greens. Tie on a big straw hat with a paper lei.

Put someone in charge of an internet search to order any kind of Hawaiian party supply you want. If on the mainland, try www.orientaltrading.com. Don't forget the little umbrellas to make your Mai Tai or fruit punch look more fun. If you have the budget, or a source for unlimited plumeria blossoms, offer a lei to each guest. If your lū'au is not in Hawai'i, then it's back to the internet for inexpensive shell or silk flower lei. A drape of bright Hawaiian fabric across the check-in table really sets the mood. Use lots of wicker and coconut baskets to hold utensils, napkins, pens and name tags.

Yes, name tags. If you have 125 people, it is likely that they won't all know each other. If they have come a long way, you can add their home city or state—it makes for good conversation. Got lots of kids in the family? Put them to work drawing a palm tree on the corner of each name tag. Coconuts are fun for the kids. Get a box of paints or magic markers and let them add a face and family name to each before they put them out on the tables.

Ask around to see who has a cousin that plays music. A great sound system with Hawaiian favorites, like the Mākaha Sons and Don Ho, is the next best thing. Your teens can burn a CD just for the party. Tell them to add in the Elvis soundtrack from Blue Hawai'i, the Hawai'i 5-0 theme music, and some Beach Boys for the over-fifty guys. Top off the mix with some really good slack key by Keola Beamer and you're set!

A lovely hula dancer makes the lū'au complete. Inviting every auntie and tūtū (grandma) to get up and dance is the finale. One nephew with an ūkulele can do magic with a party full of dancers. If your lū'au is away from the islands and you haven't had hula lessons, buy a video tape and give it a try. Remember, if you practice twice, you know more than the rest of the folks at the party.

If you have a big lū'au, you'll need a sound system. The person in charge of the food should not be thinking about the music program. Find a willing helper and appoint him or her as emcee. Make a few notes on who should be acknowledged for the decor, food, imu, and the rest. If it is a wedding, baby lū'au, retirement, or anniversary, make sure you have a list of folks who want to give a toast, roast or short speech. Give the emcee license to "use the hook" if the speech gets too long!

Welcome to Wicky-Wacky-Tiki Time

So you want to have a Wicky-Wacky-Tiki Party? It's a family birthday or an anniversary and you want the look and feel and taste of a Hawaiian lū'au without having to dig up the front yard or your condo parking lot! The good news is that Polynesian-themed party supplies are plentiful and just about anything goes for this kind of an event.

First, pick a menu that you can manage. Select recipes that have an island flavor. You don't even have to serve pork. If you want the "lū'au" taste you can follow my easy recipe for Kālua-Style Turkey. Actually, any of my backyard barbecue-style meat recipes are easy and appropriate. At a modern-day lū'au you'll usually find the teri-beef and barbecued or teri-chicken dishes for those who aren't fond of pork. My Sweet-and-Sour Chicken Breasts with Tropical Fruits or Quick and Easy Shoyu Chicken are affordable and can be doubled to feed a crowd. If you have access to a barbecue, add in some kabob-style shrimp with pineapple. Cook up some plain vegetable kabobs first, for folks who might be allergic to shellfish. Add in some cherry tomatoes and pineapple chunks for color and island taste.

In addition to the entrée meats you'll want to serve some easy dishes that feed a bunch. Plan a big tropical fruit salad or my Hilo Tropical Fruit Slaw. A standard green salad turns island-style with Balsamic Wasabi Vinaigrette. For a big crowd you could add in an Oriental Chicken Salad that can be made ahead. Parboil corn on the cob, brush it with butter and wrap it in foil. Roast it on the barbecue edges or even roast it in an oven. Bake a big pan of Sweet Potato Casserole. Make some sticky rice or fried rice. Try your hand at the laulau recipe.

Dessert, even for a big crowd, is easy. Anything with grated coconut: ice cream, sheet cake, haupia coconut milk pudding, or just plain chunks of fresh coconut cut from the shell. Hawaiian Punch is the drink of the day. Blue Hawaiians, Mai Tais and the Lava Flow can all be served with or without. After dinner, Kona coffee, of course.

Here's my hot tip: since most families don't regularly serve large groups, the serving pieces may be a challenge. Check out the rental shops where you can get the heated serving dishes, punch coolers and coffeemakers. Dig in the cupboard for baskets and cookie sheets that you can line with foil for serving. A big salad, with the Sam Choy Dressing on the side, can even be served from a cardboard box that has been covered with bright paper and lined with plastic. Dollar stores and thrift shops hold a wealth of inexpensive options for serving dishes and spoons and even decorating items.

Use party plates, cups and utensils in wild colors. Mix 'em, don't match 'em! Add in bright colored paper table coverings and napkins. Accent your table greens—any kind—with fresh pineapples and flowers. If you don't have access to fresh flowers, make big crepe paper flowers. Scatter little paper umbrellas everywhere.

For an entry area or behind the serving tables, string a fish net with glass balls. If the kids want to help, have them color and cut out big tropical fish. Hang twinkle lights behind the fish net. Wrap a post or a door in brown paper that has a big tiki face drawn on it. Lean your son's surfboard or boogie board against the wall and drape it with a silk or paper flower lei. Or cut a surfboard or two from thick cardboard or foam core. Paint them bright colors and write on them: "Surf's up" or "Hang Ten" or "Welcome To The Wicky-Wacky-Tiki Lounge." Hang bright paper streamers from everything. Add in flower lei or let the kids make paper lei for every guest. Get the CD or cassette player ready with island music.

For Ticky-Tacky fun at your Wicky-Wacky party make a note on the invitation that the loudest aloha shirt or the worst Don Ho imitation wins the prize—the entire bunch of coconuts you've painted with hula girls and palm trees! What if the winner sneaks out without the prize? Easy, plan another Wicky-Wacky-Tiki Party and make him or her the guest of honor!

Sam-Size That Dish

When you are selecting recipes for your lū'au menu, don't worry if they feed only six and you have twenty-six guests coming. You can double and double recipes as long as you watch out for a few things.

Spices, salt (sodium), pepper and "extras" like chopped onions and garlic have to be added to taste.

If a recipe calls for one table-spoon of a spice and you want to double it twice, making four full recipes, don't add four tablespoons of the spice. Add maybe one and a half or two tablespoons and then taste. Then add a little more and taste again. The same thing applies to soy sauce, oyster sauce, or hot pepper flakes. You don't want the garlic, ginger, cilantro or the onions to overpower the dish. Cornstarch or thickening is another thing to watch. Often it will take less per recipe to thicken the doubled recipes.

If the dish requires a grill or a wok, you need to think through the time it will take to actually cook four full recipes. You may want to select dishes that require less of your attention just before serving time. If the dish calls for a garnish, make sure you have doubled that as well, otherwise it will look "undressed" when you place it in the serving pans.

Remember also how many dishes you are serving. If you have only three dishes, then the servings tend to be bigger. If you have lū'au with ten different dishes, you need far less food per guest. Leftovers are fine but too much food is just a waste, except for dessert! You will never seem to have too much dessert!

Countdown to Chowdown

*Y*ou may want to consider what I call the "run through" party, a mini version of your big event. Start out with a few recipes. Cook the oven version of Kālua Pig. Add a few other dishes and invite maybe six or eight friends to try everything. When you find what works for you, you are ready to "Sam-Size It!"

2 MONTHS OUT: Make a list of all the tasks that need to be completed, the long-term jobs as well as the day-of duties. Gather family members and friends who said they would help. Find out what each one likes to do best. Pick a task-team captain for each area; i.e., location, invitations, decor, music, imu, party supplies, tents, party setup, takedown, menu, potluck coordination, beverages and ice, and cleanup. Have a budget ready. Ask for donations of tables, chairs, decorations, coolers, and other items that can be borrowed rather than rented.

Select a Location. Sign a rental contract if needed. Walk the site and make notes on everything that needs to be done. Check to make sure there are restrooms, running water, lighting or electrical plugs, parking and delivery areas, and possibly some refrigeration.

Set regular meeting times for the committees, and work out a phone tree for relaying information that doesn't require a meeting. Have each task-team give you a list of their members and contact information. Help each team make a list of advance work and day-of tasks.

Select a theme. This might be the event you are celebrating or it might be Hawaiian Nite, Hawai'i Five-Ohhhhhh!, One Paddle–Two Paddle, or Wicky-Wacky Waikīkī with Don Ho. Once you have the theme, the invitation committee can go to work on a design. Even if you personally contact all your invited guests, it is still a good idea to put the specifics on paper, along with directions, and a phone number for those who get lost.

1 MONTH OUT: Order invitations and any party supplies that have to be shipped in. Check all the addresses on the invitation list.

3 WEEKS OUT: Mail invitations. Order pig, tent or canopy materials, chairs and tables, table covers, and any catered food. Order torches for atmosphere. Order more if lighting or a power source is not available.

2 WEEKS OUT: Shop for remaining supplies, confirm all committee assignments, buy bar supplies and non-perishable foods.

1 WEEK OUT: Order flowers, lei and greens that aren't being donated.

2 DAYS OUT: Gather and deliver the imu materials if you are doing your own. Shop for remaining food.

1 DAY OUT: Pick up fish, flowers, perishable foods. Prepare any cook-ahead sauces. Load up all materials and serving pieces.

MORNING OF: Deliver everything. Dig imu at dawn. Begin setup when pig is in the imu.

6 HOURS OUT: Get all food as ready as possible. Check off all serving and eating supplies. Send someone to the store for anything that is missing.

4 HOURS OUT: Cover and decorate tables. Set up the check-in table and gift table if gifts are expected. Lay out name tags and pens if the crowd doesn't know each other.

2 HOURS OUT: Cook the last-minute dishes.

1 HOUR OUT: Take a deep breath. Get a vision in your mind of the party in full swing. See the kids playing, the aunties talking, the musicians rocking out, everyone having all the fun you have planned for so long. Put on your clean aloha shirt and get ready to greet your guests.

PARTY TIME: Light the torches. Cue the musicians. Open the imu. Lift the pig, set out the food, give the pule (blessing) and dig in!

PART TWO
Recipes

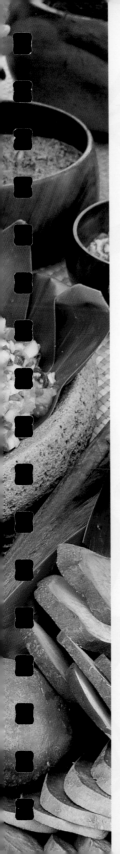

The Hawaiian-Style Lū'au

Succulent pig, fish wrapped in ti leaves, savory ethnic dishes, poke, poi, rice – the menu for a lū'au, especially a big one, can go on and on. Lū'au tables these days feature a wide variety of foods, in almost any combination. But the good-old fashioned Hawaiian lū'au calls to mind something more traditional, an array of dishes that are standbys, tried and true, for those of us who grew up in the islands.

I have gathered here some of those dishes. Included are a few of my own sentimental favorites, specialties from my own mom's kitchen, and standards ranging from hearty poi to delicate mahimahi. You can create your own mouth-watering feast by choosing and combining some of these, but don't be shy about finding your own variations to enrich and enhance the mix!

Steamed Mahimahi Laulau

Makes 4 Servings

Using a steaming method is a good way to cook this moist, delicate fish. It helps retain the moisture, texture, and fresh flavor of this great-tasting, mild white fish.

2 cups finely julienned carrots
2 cups finely julienned zucchini
1 cup shiitake sliced mushrooms
8 tī leaves
12 fresh mahimahi fillets (2 ounces each) (don't substitute any other fish)
salt and pepper to taste
enough string to tie each laulau

HERB SAUCE

1-1/2 cups mayonnaise
1 tablespoon soy sauce
1 tablespoon fresh dill, chopped

※ Mix carrots and zucchini together and divide into four equal portions. Divide mushrooms into four equal portions. Mix herb sauce ingredients and set aside. Remove hard rib from tī leaves to make flexible, or cook leaves on high in microwave for 1 minute to soften.

※ To build each laulau, first make a tī leaf cross on the table by laying one tī leaf over another at right angles. Sprinkle vegetable mix in the center, then lay a mahi fillet on top of the vegetables. Spread a thin layer of herb sauce on fish and sprinkle with more vegetables. Place another fillet on top, spread with herb sauce, sprinkle with vegetables. Finish with a third fillet that is topped with herb sauce, vegetable mix, and a sprinkle of mushrooms. Season with salt and pepper to taste.

※ Gather up tī leaves to make a purse around fish and tie tightly with string just above bundle. Repeat for all four portions, using a fourth of the vegetables, a fourth of the mushrooms, and three mahi fillets for each laulau. Steam for 8 to 10 minutes.

Assorted Seafood Laulau

Makes 1 Serving

Mahimahi, scallops and shrimp all become close friends in Sam's laulau. The soy-mayonnaise mixture, layered between the fish and vegetables, is rich and moist. Scallops and shrimp are added at the top. Steam for the proper time, bring out the poi and eat them.

1 quart water
6 tablespoons mayonnaise
2 teaspoons soy sauce
1 teaspoon chopped dill
salt and pepper to taste
2 tī leaves
3 (2-1/2 ounce) pieces of fresh fish (mahimahi or salmon are best)
4 bay scallops, rinsed and shelled
4 bay shrimp, peeled and deveined
1/2 cup fresh spinach leaves
1/2 cup carrots, julienned
1/2 cup zucchini, julienned
2 fresh shiitake mushrooms, rinsed and sliced
other assorted seafood (optional)

❧ In a small bowl, combine mayonnaise, soy sauce, fresh dill, salt and pepper. Mix well. Set aside.

❧ Take two medium-size tī leaves and, with a sharp knife, remove the ribs. Then with tip of knife, barely tap the rib midway. Pull the rib completely off of two tī leaves. On one of the leaves, split the stem to the bottom of the leaf.

❧ Crisscross the two leaves to make the base of the laulau. Begin layering laulau with one piece of fish, then a dollop of mayonnaise-soy sauce mix, followed by zucchini, carrots, spinach, and a couple of slices of shiitake mushrooms. Repeat the process two more times, stacking the fish and other items. At the very top, add the bay shrimp and scallops and whatever other kind of seafood you desire. Pulling the stems up, wrap the split stems around the other two stems and in a knot so that a pouch is formed.

so Place a steaming rack in a 4-quart pot along with 1/2 to 1 quart of water. Heat until water is at a rapid boil. Carefully place laulau in a pot and cover. Steam for approximately 15 to 20 minutes, or until done.

so Carefully remove laulau and serve with rice or poi.

Easy Chicken Laulau

Makes 4 Servings

This is a traditional Hawaiian dish that goes back thousands of years. You cook it in a steamer basket instead of an underground oven, though. It's not hard to do and is very good and good for you—real moist and flavorful, with healthy ingredients.

4 boneless chicken breasts
2 ounces salted butterfish
1 tablespoon Hawaiian salt
20 lūʻau (taro) leaves (or fresh spinach leaves)
8 tī leaves for wrappers (or corn husks, or tin foil)
enough string to tie wrappers around laulau

so Leave chicken breasts whole. It tastes better to leave the skin on, but you can remove it if you'd like. Sprinkle chicken with salt. Cut fish into four equal pieces.

so Rinse lūʻau leaves, trim stems, remove larger veins. Remove part of back rib of each tī leaf so the leaves become pliable (or cook tī leaves in microwave on high for a minute or so, to make them flexible). (Tī leaves may be obtained from a florist if you don't have any growing in your yard.) Divide lūʻau leaves into four piles of five each, with the largest leaf on the bottom of the pile. If you are using spinach in place of lūʻau leaves, it won't be as flavorful, but will still be good. You may have to use more spinach leaves because they are smaller.

so Place a chicken breast and a piece of butterfish on each pile of leaves and sprinkle with a little salt, if desired. Gathering up the lūʻau leaves around the chicken and fish, wrap into a tight bundle and place bundle in the middle of two tī leaves you have laid over each other in the form of a cross. The bundle should be placed directly in the center of the cross. Gather up the tī leaves and tie

The Hawaiian-Style Lūʻau

tightly with string just above bundle to make a purse, securing the laulau inside.

🔊 Place in steamer and steam for 1 hour and 45 minutes. Check occasionally to make sure there's enough water in the steamer.

🔊 To serve, remove laulau from tī leaves and discard tī leaves.

* See page 52 for safety information about lū'au leaves.

Chicken and Mahimahi Laulau

Makes 4 Servings

Practice is what makes this perfect. Learn how to do a perfect laulau wrap. The layering of the ingredients is the first secret. The second is how they are placed in the crisscrossed tī leaves. And, the third secret is steaming them correctly. They are best served with rice or poi.

1 quart water
8 tī leaves
1 bunch fresh spinach
4 skinless, boneless chicken breast halves
salt to taste
4 mahimahi fillets (3 ounces each), sliced thinly
1/2 cup julienned carrots
1/2 cup julienned zucchini
1/4 cup medium-diced sweet potato
1/2 cup medium-diced taro
1/4 cup rinsed and julienned fresh shiitake mushrooms
4 slices tomato

🔊 Take two medium-size tī leaves and, with a sharp knife, remove the ribs. Then with tip of knife, barely "tap" the rib midway. Pull the rib completely off of two tī leaves. On one of the leaves, split the stem to the bottom of the leaf.

🔊 Crisscross the two leaves to make the base of the laualu. Begin layering laualu with spinach leaves, chicken breast, salt, mahimahi fillet, carrot and zucchini mixture, sweet potatoes, taro, shiitake mushrooms and top with a slice of tomato. Pulling the stems up, wrap the split stems around the other two stems in a knot so that a pouch is formed.

∞ Place a steaming rack in a 4-quart pot along with 1/2 to 1 quart of water. Heat until water is at a rapid boil. Carefully place laulau in pot and cover. Steam for approximately 30 to 45 minutes or until done.

∞ Carefully remove laulau and serve with rice or poi.

Great taste and naturally low in fat.

Poi—From Scratch

Makes 12 Servings

You must have poi with your lūʻau whether you like it or not. It just isn't like a lūʻau without it. Poi has been a Hawaiian staple for thousands of years. It is very nutritious and good for you, and, if you sample it often enough, you will eventually acquire a taste for it—maybe. If you're not used to it, it's best to eat it when it's very fresh, although some people like it better after it has sat around for a few days and becomes sour.

I don't recommend making poi yourself, as it's a lot of work and very time-consuming, and you can't beat the commercial variety.

Commercial poi comes in various forms, the most popular being the type sold in plastic bags. All you need to do to get the poi ready to eat is add a third cup or so of water to the bag, seal the top and mix by kneading the bag. When the poi is smooth, pour it into individual serving bowls.

If you're feeling ambitious, you can try making poi from scratch.

3 pounds taro corms, peeled, boiled and diced into 1-inch cubes
3 cups water

∞ Mash boiled taro in a wooden bowl with a wooden potato masher until you've turned it into a thick paste. Little by little, work in the water with your hands, then force the poi through several layers of cheesecloth to remove lumps and fiber.

∞ Serve it fresh, or let it ferment for that distinctive sour taste by allowing it to stand for two to three days in a cool place.

The Hawaiian-Style Lūʻau

Kālua-Style Turkey
with Dried Fruit and Oyster Stuffing
and Baked Taro and Sweet Potatoes

No need to dig up the front lawn, this kālua turkey does just fine in the oven. The stuffing is a "Sam special." Serve it with the baked taro and sweet potatoes and you have a real holiday feast.

Dried Fruit and Oyster Stuffing (see recipe below)
Baked Taro and Sweet Potatoes (see recipe on
  following page)
1 whole turkey with giblets (about 15 pounds)
Hawaiian salt to taste
1/4 cup soy sauce
2 tablespoons liquid smoke
2 quarts chicken stock or low-sodium chicken broth
10 medium-size tī leaves

🔊 Preheat oven to 350°F.

🔊 Wash turkey, pat dry inside and out. Rub with soy sauce and season generously with salt and pepper. Place half the tī leaves in a roasting pan, add liquid smoke and chicken stock to the pan, add the turkey, breast down, to the pan and cover with remaining tī leaves. Seal pan very well with foil. Bake for about 4 hours, or until done (depending on turkey size). After turkey cools, shred the meat off the bone.

DRIED FRUIT AND OYSTER STUFFING
Makes About 8 Cups

Begin with bacon for flavor and for the great aroma of the bacon and the onions cooking in the pan. Add several dried fruits. Cranberries add the festive look. The oysters should be poached a bit then added in. The sweet bread gives 'ono flavor.

1/4 pound bacon
1/4 cup chopped onion
1/4 cup chopped carrots
1/4 cup chopped celery

1/4 cup peeled garlic cloves
1/4 cup minced fresh thyme
turkey giblets
1 pound assorted dried fruit (cranberry, mango, papaya)
1 quart chicken stock or low-sodium chicken broth
1 quart oyster meat in juice
2 cups toasted Hawaiian sweet bread cubes
   (about 1/2-inch pieces)
salt and pepper to taste

€ Render the bacon and sauté the onion, carrots, celery, garlic and thyme. When vegetables are cooked, add the giblets and dried fruits. Cook for 5 minutes. Add the chicken stock and oysters (lightly poach oyster meat in juice before adding to stock). When hot, add the sweet bread (for a drier stuffing add less stock). Cook until all the liquid is absorbed, season with salt and pepper to taste.

BAKED TARO AND SWEET POTATOES
Makes About 12 Cups

This dish is good any time of year. Butter the pan, layer the taro and sweet potato, dot with more butter. Add raisins, more butter, macadamia nuts and more butter. Drizzle with coconut syrup and add just a bit more butter!

1 pound whole butter
3 pounds taro, peeled and thinly sliced
3 pounds sweet potato, peeled and thinly sliced
1/2 cup packed brown sugar
1 cup raisins
salt and pepper to taste
1/2 cup all-purpose flour
1/2 cup chopped macadamia nuts
4 ounces coconut syrup

€ Preheat oven to 350°F. Rub a casserole dish with butter and layer the taro and sweet potatoes, dotting with butter, brown sugar, raisins, salt and pepper. When done, combine the flour, macadamia nuts, butter, and coconut syrup until it is dry and resembles crumbly pie dough. When taro and sweet potatoes are done, top with the macadamia nut mixture and bake for 30 to 40 minutes until it is golden brown.

No-Imu Kālua Pig

The traditional way to cook a whole pig Hawaiian-style is an underground oven, or imu. It's a lot of work and it takes all day long, but, man, does it taste good. Lots of people still do it that way for parties and special events, but you can also do it in your oven with a lot less hassle, and it tastes almost as good.

8 pounds pork butt
4 tablespoons liquid smoke
4 tablespoons Hawaiian salt
8 to 12 large tī leaves, ribs removed (see "About Tī Leaves")

🔊 Preheat oven to 350°F. After scoring pork on all sides with 1/4-inch deep slits about an inch apart, rub with salt, then liquid smoke. Wrap the pork completely in tī leaves, tie with string, and wrap with foil.

🔊 Place meat in a shallow roasting pan with 2 cups water and roast for 4 hours.

🔊 Dissolve 1 tablespoon Hawaiian salt in 2 cups boiling water and add a few drops of liquid smoke. Shred the cooked pork and let stand in this solution for a few minutes before serving.

ABOUT TĪ LEAVES

Tī leaves come from a woody plant of the agave family—*Cordyline australis*. They are used extensively in Polynesia as a wrap for food. In this recipe, they are not necessary for the success of this dish. But if you can obtain them, they will add an authentic flavor to your kālua pig.

Kālua Pig and Cabbage

Life is busy for most of us so anything that makes cooking simpler is a great idea. One of those for me is my crockpot. I can throw stuff in it in the morning before things get hectic and by dinner the house is smelling scrumptious and dinner is ready to be served.

2 to 3 pounds pork butt (or pork shoulder as it's labeled here)
3 tablespoons liquid smoke—more if you like stronger flavor (found in a bottle by the bbq and hot sauces, mesquite is more mellow, hickory is stronger)
3 tablespoons Hawaiian salt—more or less to taste (or kosher salt if no more Hawaiian kine)
water to fill crockpot 1/2 way after pork is inside

∞ Cook 4 to 6 hours on high or 8 to 10 hours on low in a crockpot. Remove pork and shred with fork. Place cut-up cabbage in broth and cook on high until tender to liking. Put all together and serve.

Straight Hawaiian-Style 'Inamona Poke

Taste of old—this recipe is simple, straightforward. It definitely brings back a lot of memories of my old days picking limu (seaweed) from certain parts of the ocean and Hukilau Bay.

1 pound very fresh raw aku (skipjack tuna), 'ahi
   (yellowfin tuna) or other fish, cut in bite-size cubes
1 small ball limu kohu (edible red seaweed, about
   1/2 cup, chopped)
'inamona (roasted, crushed, kukui nut, about 1 teaspoon
   to taste) (see "About 'Inamona and Limu Kohu")
1 Hawaiian red chili pepper, minced
salt to taste

℥ Rinse and chop limu kohu. In a mixing bowl, combine all ingredients.

ABOUT 'INAMONA AND LIMU KOHU

These two traditional Hawaiian ingredients may be a bit hard to obtain outside of Hawai'i. Fortunately, the World Wide Web is proving to be a good source, even for obscure items like these. It is strongly recommended that you obtain the limu kohu for this recipe, as there isn't a good substitute for this ingredient.

'Inamona is a condiment made of salted kukui nuts (candlenuts). You can substitute 1-1/2 teaspoons cashew nuts, roasted, crushed and salted for the quantity of 'inamona in this recipe.

Limu kohu is a fine-textured red seaweed (*Asparagopsis taxiformus*) that adds a faint iodine scent to the dishes it flavors.

My Mom's Squid Lū'au

Lū'au leaves, which are the leaves from the taro plant, are very high in oxalic acid. Simmering them for an hour is necessary to make them safe to eat. Do not reduce the cooking time for this step. Baking soda also serves to neutralize the acid.

2 pounds calamari
3 pounds lū'au leaves
1 tablespoon Hawaiian salt
1/2 teaspoon baking soda
6 tablespoons butter
2 medium onions, diced
3 cups coconut milk
1-1/2 teaspoons salt
1 tablespoon sugar

&) Clean calamari and slice in rings, then set aside.

&) Wash lū'au leaves, and remove stems and thick veins. In a pot boil 3 cups of water with the Hawaiian salt and baking soda. Add the leaves to the boiling water and reduce heat. Simmer, partially covered, for 1 hour. Drain and squeeze out liquid.

&) Sauté onions and calamari in butter until the onions are translucent. Add the coconut milk, cooked lū'au leaves, salt and sugar. Simmer for 30 minutes.

Chicken Lū'au—
My Mother's Favorite

Makes 8 (1/2-cup) Side Dish Servings

My mom taught me how to do this. Every year we have a big Hawaiian lū'au and the chicken lū'au has to be done the Choy family way.

1 pound lū'au (young taro leaves—see Note)
3 cups water
1 tablespoon Hawaiian (sea) salt
1/2 teaspoon baking soda
3/4 pound skinless, boneless chicken breast, cubed
2 tablespoons butter
1/2 medium onion, chopped
1 cup chicken stock
1 cup coconut milk
1/2 teaspoon salt

🍃 Rinse lū'au and trim off stems and thick veins. In a stockpot, bring water, Hawaiian salt and baking soda to a boil. Add lū'au and cook partially covered for 1 hour. Drain off and squeeze out excess liquid.

🍃 In a large saucepan, heat butter and sauté onions until translucent. Add chicken and cook 3 minutes, stirring frequently. Add chicken stock, coconut milk, cooked lū'au and salt. Simmer for 20 minutes or until chicken is cooked.

NOTE: Can substitute fresh spinach, which does not need pre-cooking.

Chicken Long Rice

This is an acquired taste. Kids joke that it looks like worms. Once you savor this dish with the chicken and shredded vegetables, accompanied by some fresh poi, green onions and Hawaiian salt, you will never pass it by again, no matter what the kids say!

4 ounces long rice (see "About Long Rice")
20 dried shiitake mushrooms
4 cups chicken broth
2 pounds skinless, boneless chicken, cubed
2-inch finger of fresh ginger, crushed
1 medium onion, minced
2 cups thinly sliced celery
2 carrots, julienned
6 green onions, cut in 1-inch lengths

๛ Soak long rice in warm water for 1 hour. Soak mushrooms in warm water for 20 minutes and drain. Remove stems and slice caps.

๛ Pour chicken broth into a large pot, add chicken and ginger and simmer for 5 minutes. Add onion, celery, carrots, and mushrooms, and simmer for another 4 to 5 minutes.

๛ Drain long rice and cut into 3-inch lengths. Add long rice and green onions to the pot and stir. Cook for an additional 5 minutes or until long rice becomes translucent.

ABOUT LONG RICE

Long rice, also known as bean threads or cellophane noodles, is made from mung beans. These are available in Chinese markets, and look like bundles of thin, hard translucent white noodles. Long rice has very little flavor of its own—but will easily absorb flavor of other ingredients. Once soaked, the noodles become soft and gelatinous. Take care not to overcook them—so they don't become mushy.

Traditional Lomilomi Salmon

Makes 24 Servings

Here in Hawai'i the lū'au is the traditional way of celebrating a special occasion. On any given weekend, you will find lū'au going on all over. They are held for birthdays, anniversaries, weddings, grand openings of new businesses, blessings of boats, the opening or closing of a special event, and for any other reason somebody feels like celebrating. And we're not talking pūpū or crackers and cheese—this is heavy eating, true feasting. It's a tradition in Hawai'i to hold a baby lū'au on your child's first birthday, as a way of giving thanks that your baby made it through the first year. Anywhere from 50 to 5,000 people will show up for one of these baby lū'au, and it's really festive, with Hawaiian entertainment and endless food, and it can go on for two or three days. I learned to cook as a kid helping my dad cater lū'au in Lā'ie. I've included only a few of my favorite recipes here; a big lū'au will have many additional dishes.

4 cups diced salted salmon
12 tomatoes, diced
4 small red onions, diced
1 cup thinly sliced green onion
1 to 2 Hawaiian chili peppers, or 1/4 teaspoon red pepper
   flakes (optional)

🍓 Combine all ingredients and mix well. Serve well chilled. (Salted salmon comes with various degrees of saltiness, so it's a good idea to taste it before making this dish. If it's too salty, you need to soak it overnight in enough water to cover, and then rinse it twice before using.)

Haupia (Coconut Pudding)

This simple but delicious pudding goes way back to the old days when the Hawaiians had only fruit, coconuts, and wild sugar cane for sweets.

3 cups frozen coconut milk, thawed (or 2 cups fresh
 coconut milk mixed with 1 cup water)
1/2 cup sugar
1/2 cup cornstarch
1/2 teaspoon vanilla
pinch of salt

🍥 In a saucepan, combine coconut milk and sugar. Gradually mix in cornstarch. Add vanilla and salt. Stir and cook on medium heat until thickened. Pour into an oiled 9-inch square pan. Chill for at least 1 hour. Cut into 36 squares.

Pūpū

*T*icklish, that's what a pūpū is. It tickles the palate. It says, "Get ready for what's coming." A pūpū can be elegant, like Deep-Fried Mahimahi Macadamia Nut Fingers, or a simple poke with limu, onion, soy sauce, and red pepper.

If you are doing your own lūʻau cooking, select some of my make-ahead pūpū that are ready to serve when the guests arrive. If your plan is potluck-style, assign the pūpū course to several folks and you undoubtedly will be delighted with their well-rounded pūpū selection. If some of the pūpū need to be served chilled, just fill a big bowl with ice and put a smaller pūpū serving bowl in the center. No worries on the melting factor. The pūpū will be gone before the ice!

'Ahi Tartare with Ginger

The meat of the 'ahi oxidizes when exposed to air, and changes from a delicious red to a brown color in a matter of days. For this reason, the 'ahi is usually not filleted until shortly before use. Make sure to pick the freshest fish for this tartare appetizer.

Place heaping tablespoons of the tartare mixture in separate clumps on a bed of organic field greens, then lightly sprinkle black sesame seeds on the very top of each clump. To make it pretty, arrange edible flowers around the platter. It's a beautiful presentation. Really impressive.

1-1/2 pounds fresh 'ahi fillet
2 tablespoons sesame oil
2 tablespoons mirin (Japanese sweet rice wine)
1 tablespoon rice vinegar
1/2 cup minced green onion
1/2 tablespoon minced fresh ginger
salt and pepper to taste

GARNISH

organic field greens
edible flowers
black goma (black sesame seeds)

🍴 Mince the 'ahi with a very sharp knife. Place it in a glass or wooden bowl. Add the sesame oil, mirin, rice vinegar, green onion, and ginger. Mix well. Season with salt and pepper to taste. Refrigerate.

Poke Patties

This is like tartare, except we cut the fish in tiny cubes and make a patty similar to a hamburger. We sear it, yet on the inside it's rare, with poke-style seasoning.

panko (packaged Japanese-style fine bread crumbs) or
    Italian bread crumbs
2 tablespoons canola oil
2 tablespoons chopped fresh ogo (edible seaweed)
2 tablespoons soy sauce
1 teaspoon sesame oil
pinch each salt, pepper

PATTIES

1 cup diced very fresh 'ahi (yellowfin tuna) or aku
    (skipjack tuna), cut in about 1/4- to 3/8-inch cubes
1/4 cup minced onion
1/4 cup minced green onion
1 egg

SAUCE

1/4 cup sliced mushrooms
2 tablespoons butter
1 teaspoon soy sauce
1 teaspoon oyster sauce
1 teaspoon chopped cilantro

₳ Combine patty ingredients and form two patties. Press patties and panko to coat. In frying pan, heat oil over medium-high heat. Gently place patties in pan and brown both sides, keeping the inside of the patties medium-rare.

₳ To make sauce, sauté mushrooms in butter for 2 minutes. Add remaining sauce ingredients and cook for 1 minute. Pour sauce over patties and serve as pūpū, or appetizers.

Deep-Fried Mahimahi Macadamia Nut Fingers

Makes 12 (4-Piece) Servings

This elegant pūpū features all the foods that capture the essence of the Islands—mahimahi, macadamia nuts, pineapple, papaya, even cane sugar.

3 pounds mahimahi (dolphinfish) fillets,
   cut in 2-by-3-inch pieces
1-1/2 cups minced macadamia nuts
vegetable oil for deep-frying, such as safflower,
   cottonseed or corn oil
Tropical Marmalade (see recipe on following page)

MARINADE

2 or 3 eggs
1 stalk green onion, minced
1 tablespoon minced fresh ginger
1 tablespoon soy sauce
1 teaspoon sherry
1 teaspoon sugar
1 teaspoon cornstarch
salt and white pepper to taste

ᔥ In a large mixing bowl, combine marinade ingredients and marinate mahimahi "fingers" for 10 minutes; drain. Dip fish pieces in macadamia nuts to coat.

ᔥ In a frying pan, heat oil on medium-high heat. Fry fish fingers a few at a time until golden. Drain briefly on paper towels and serve. Serve these nutty morsels with Tropical Marmalade.

COOKING TIP: Roast macadamia nut bits on a dry baking sheet in a preheated 300°F oven for 3 or 4 minutes until lightly browned.

TROPICAL MARMALADE
Makes 1 Cup

2 cups diced fresh pineapple
3 cups diced fresh papaya
1/2 cup fresh pohā berries (cape gooseberries)
6 tablespoons sugar or to taste
chopped fresh mint or spearmint
1/8 teaspoon peppered horseradish or to taste (optional)

⅋ In a saucepan, combine all ingredients except mint or spearmint. Bring to a boil, then simmer—stirring every 5 minutes to avoid scorching—for 1 hour or until mixture reaches jam consistency. Cool. Then fold in "Sam Choy's twist"—the fresh mint or spearmint.

Pipi kaula (Dried Beef)

Makes About 8 Servings

Pipi kaula is a beef, salted and dried in the sun, then broiled before eating. The literal translation of this Hawaiian word is "rope beef." This was a saddlebag staple for the paniolo (cowboy) as they rode the sloped pastures of upcountry Maui and the Kohala area of the Big Island.

1-1/2 pounds beef tenderloin
2 tablespoons salt, preferably sea salt
1/2 cup soy sauce
1/2 teaspoon sugar
2 tablespoons lemon juice

⅋ Pound to tenderize the beef and cut into pieces 4 inches long, 2 inches wide, and 3/4-inch thick. Sprinkle with salt, soy sauce, and lemon juice. Dry in the sun for several days, taking care to screen the meat from dust and flies (a screened box was traditionally used for beef and fish). Makes 3/4 pounds dried beef.

Spicy Chicken Wingettes

This is a great finger food. It's easy to prepare, and even easier to eat. Great for parties. And very addictive. You can't eat just one or two or three. I'd like to say it's "finger lickin' good," but I know I'd better not.

1/2 cup soy sauce
1/2 teaspoon white pepper
1 tablespoon minced garlic
1/2 teaspoon minced fresh ginger
1 cup sherry
one large bag chicken wing drummettes (about 3 pounds)
1 cup flour
1/2 cup rice flour
1/2 cup cornstarch
enough oil or fat for deep-frying

℘ In a large bowl, mix together the soy sauce, white pepper, garlic, ginger and sherry. Add chicken to soy sauce mixture and marinate for 1 hour. Mix together flour, rice flour and cornstarch and set aside. Remove chicken from marinade and dredge in flour mixture until coated, or shake the pieces in a plastic bag containing flour mixture.

℘ Heat oil to 350°F to 375°F. Deep-fry chicken for about 3 or 4 minutes until golden brown. After frying, you don't need to drain the chicken because it goes into the sauce.

SAUCE

2 cups soy sauce
1 cup water
1 cup pineapple juice
1-1/2 cups sugar
1 cup minced scallions
1 teaspoon minced fresh ginger
1 tablespoon hot pepper flakes
1 tablespoon sesame seed oil

ᔑᓍ In a large mixing bowl add all the ingredients and whisk until all the sugar is dissolved. (You can make the sauce a day ahead of time, if you like.)

ᔑᓍ Place the hot chicken wings in the sauce for about half a minute, remove and arrange on a serving platter over a bed of sprouts or lettuce leaves. It goes great with the vegetable roll-up platter.

Spring Rolls

Season to taste....some like it saltier than others.

1 pound ground pork
1 pound shrimp, shelled, deveined, ground
1 onion, chopped
little bit garlic, minced
carrots, shredded
long rice
shiitake mushrooms
egg yolks (save the whites to seal wrappers)
salt
pepper
little bit sugar
about 75 lumpia wrappers
oil for deep-frying

ᔑᓍ Mix everything together and spoon about 1 teaspoon into the middle of a wrapper. Roll it up, seal with the egg whites, and deep fry till golden brown. Sample one to make sure the pork is fully cooked.

ᔑᓍ You can use the same filling to stuff bittermelons. Clean out the seeds first, parboil small kine, stuff it, then cook it in chicken broth till the pork is cooked.

Teriyaki Roll-ups

Island marinade, with papaya, garlic, ginger, soy, brown sugar and sherry, turns the steak butter-tender. Now, roll it around the vegetables and grill. No barbecue? A wok will work, too.

3/4 cup chopped onions
2 tablespoons minced fresh garlic
2 tablespoons peeled and minced fresh ginger
1 tablespoon brown sugar
1-1/2 cups soy sauce
1 cup water
1/2 papaya, seeded, peeled and mashed
2 tablespoons sherry
1 pound flank steak, sliced into thin sheets
2 teaspoons vegetable oil
1/2 cup julienned carrots
1/2 cup julienned green beans
2 tablespoons chopped green onions
1/4 cup julienned red bell peppers
salt and pepper to taste

🔊 To prepare marinade, combine onions, garlic, ginger, brown sugar, soy sauce, water, papaya, and sherry in a large bowl and mix well. Marinate flank steak overnight in refrigerator.

🔊 In a large skillet, sauté remaining vegetables over medium-high heat until al dente. Lay a thin sheet of steak on a clean flat surface (like a plate). Spoon vegetables onto one side of the flank steak, season with salt and pepper. Roll the meat and secure it with toothpicks. Grill meat until cooked.

NOTE: Meat rolls can be grilled in a large hot skillet, a wok or over a hibachi or barbecue.

Da Kine Poke Supreme

It can take a while to round up all the ingredients for this poke. But, the mixture is so good, it's worth the effort.

2 cups cubed raw 'ahi
1 cup 'opihi, or poached scallops, or cooked mussels
6 whole crabs, cleaned and lightly salted, quartered
2 pounds octopus, thinly sliced
1/2 cup chopped ogo
1 cup coarsely chopped limu wawae'iole (rat's feet
   seaweed or miru)
2 tomatoes, chopped
2 cups chopped cucumbers
1 cup chopped onion
6 tablespoons soy sauce
2 teaspoons sesame oil
1 teaspoon red pepper flakes, or 1 Hawaiian chili pepper

ဆ Mix ingredients well and chill until ice-cold.

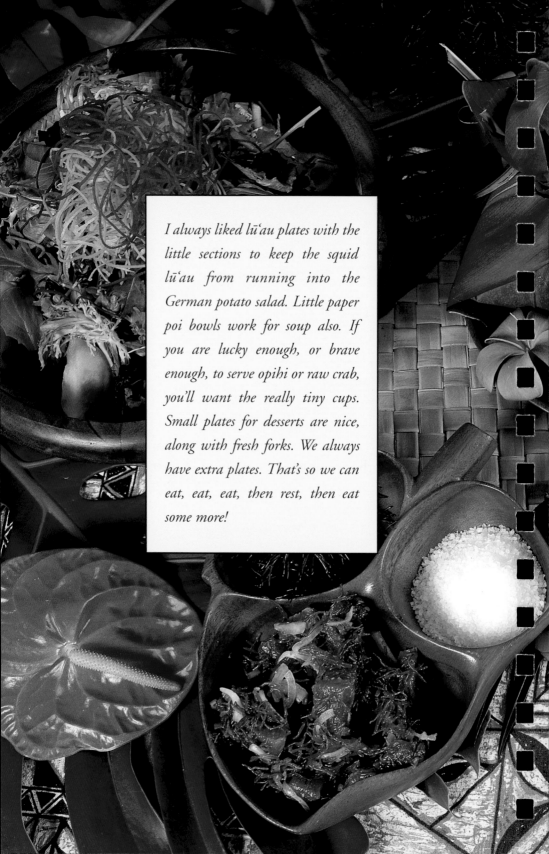

I always liked lūʻau plates with the little sections to keep the squid lūʻau from running into the German potato salad. Little paper poi bowls work for soup also. If you are lucky enough, or brave enough, to serve opihi or raw crab, you'll want the really tiny cups. Small plates for desserts are nice, along with fresh forks. We always have extra plates. That's so we can eat, eat, eat, then rest, then eat some more!

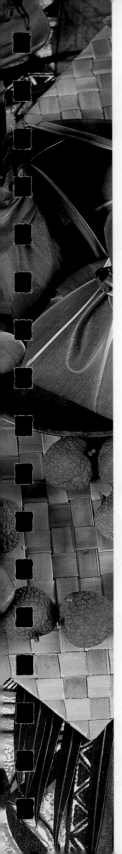

Salads

We all know that a salad can be a whole meal. For the lūʻau menu you'll want your salad section to look more like a buffet table with lots of choices. The salad section also is the place to tuck in some olives, pickles and pickled mango for accompaniment. Title cards here should identify anything with shellfish—insurance against any allergic reactions.

To keep things cold, line a long flat box with a couple of silver gray or green, heavy-duty, plastic bags. Push the bags down into the box and wrap the extra up and over the edge to cover the box. Fill the box with ice, decorate the edges with ferns and tī leaves and settle the bowls of salad into the ice. You've now made a disposable "chill tray!"

'Ahi Poke Salad

We've taken poke to new levels and developed some interesting salads. This one represents an innovation which has been well received all over.

1/2 cup canola oil
2 (10-inch) wheat-flour tortillas
4 ounces very fresh 'ahi (yellowfin tuna),
    cut in 1-inch cubes
1 tablespoon chopped onion
1 tablespoon chopped green onion
1 tablespoon chopped fresh ogo (edible seaweed)
2 tablespoons soy sauce
1 tablespoon sesame oil
1 handful mixed fresh salad greens
1/2 cup cooked somen (Japanese thin white
    wheat noodles)

₭ In a frying pan, heat oil on medium-high heat. Fry tortillas, one at a time, until golden brown; blot with paper towels to remove excess oil.

₭ Prepare poke by combining 'ahi, onions, ogo, soy sauce and sesame oil; mix well.

₭ To assemble salad, layer on plate one tortilla followed by greens, the other tortilla, somen and poke.

Hilo Tropical Fruit Slaw

Makes 8 (1-Cup) Servings

At the Hilo Open Market you can see all the fresh fruits. So I brought out a file recipe and created a slaw using the fruits. This is ideal with broiled chicken breast.

1 Puna papaya, seeded, peeled and thinly sliced
1 cup peeled and thinly sliced Lāna'i pineapple
1 medium mango, peeled and thinly sliced
1 star fruit, ribs trimmed, thinly sliced and seeded
1 kiwi fruit, peeled and thinly sliced
6 Waimea strawberries, hulled and quartered
1/2 cup whole pohā berries (cape gooseberries)
1 Big Island banana, sliced
1 medium head radicchio, leaves separated

HILO TROPICAL FRUIT SLAW DRESSING
Makes 2 Servings

1 ripe Puna papaya, seeded and peeled
1/2 cup plain yogurt
2 tablespoons honey
1/4 teaspoon EACH salt, white pepper

ᕲ Machine-process dressing ingredients for 30 seconds.

ᕲ In a large salad bowl, combine fruits and fold in prepared dressing. Serve on radicchio leaves.

Pacific Rim Potato Salad

Makes 18 (1/2-Cup) Servings

We've got all different things in this salad—crab, uncooked corn kernels that add a little crunchiness. Whew, 'ono. You never had it like that before?

2 pounds new Red B (round red boiling) potatoes
2 cups shredded crabmeat
1/2 cup bay shrimps
4 hard-boiled eggs, chopped
1 cup fresh corn kernels
1/2 cup pitted medium-size black olives
1/4 cup sliced water chestnuts
1-1/2 cups chopped fresh spinach
1/2 cup minced Maui onion
1/2 cup minced celery
1/2 cup grated carrots
2-1/2 cups mayonnaise
salt and pepper to taste

❧ Cook potatoes in lightly salted boiling water until fork-tender. Cool, then cut into eighths.

❧ In a large mixing bowl, toss all ingredients lightly to combine. Adjust seasoning with salt and pepper, if necessary.

Hawaiian Barbecued Shrimp Salad
with Papaya/Pineapple Marmalade

Makes 4 Servings

This is one of my all-time most popular recipes. It's also very simple to make.

You can't get much simpler than this: fresh whole shrimp with tails and heads on, marinated, then cooked quickly on the hibachi. Throw the shrimp on the top of salad greens and marinated somen noodles and, man, you got a winner.

1 pound jumbo shrimp (16 to 20 count)
4 flour tortillas
8 to 12 ounces Japanese somen noodles
1 medium head iceberg lettuce, finely julienned
1 cup bean sprouts
1 grated carrot
2 radishes, thinly sliced
2 cups finely chopped napa cabbage or won bok
1/2 cup diagonally sliced long strips green onions
4 to 8 wedges of fresh pineapple
4 to 8 wedges of fresh papaya
sprigs of cilantro for garnish

ॐ Rinse shrimp. Cut the top shell, but not all the way through, because you're going to leave the shell on for the festive look. Peel shell from shrimp like a fan, leaving shell and tail attached at tail end. Devein shrimp. Combine marinade ingredients and blend well. Remove 4 tablespoons of marinade and set aside to mix with noodles. Marinate shrimp for 30 minutes.

ॐ Deep-fry flour tortillas and drain on paper towels. Set aside. Cook noodles according to package directions, rinse, and mix 4 tablespoons of marinade, then place in fridge until chilled, about 20 to 30 minutes.

In a large bowl, combine lettuce, bean sprouts, grated carrot, sliced radishes, chopped napa cabbage, green onion, and mix well. Cut fresh pineapple and papayas into wedges, removing core and seeds.

When everything is ready, place shrimp on barbecue or under broiler and cook for 3 to 5 minutes, turning once.

Build each salad by first placing deep-fried tortilla on the plate, adding a couple handfuls of colorful salad mix, then chilled somen noodles, then 1/4 of the shrimp on top, and garnishing with a sprig or two of cilantro.

Place the wedges of pineapple and papaya around the edge of plate, alternating with dollops of Papaya/Pineapple Marmalade.

I like my Creamy Oriental dressing with this salad, but you can use the dressing of your choice.

PAPAYA/PINEAPPLE MARMALADE

1/2 cup diced papaya
1/2 cup diced pineapple
3 tablespoons sugar

In a saucepan, cook fruit and sugar for 20 minutes. Serve warm, or cold.

Oriental Macadamia Nut Chicken Salad
with Fried Noodles

Makes 4 Servings

Take a piece of chicken, marinate it, cover it with macadamia nuts, deep-fry it, or pan-fry it, and serve it with fried noodles on mixed salad greens and one of our signature dressings, and you have yourself a surprisingly elegant, simple-to-prepare, and very satisfying salad.

4 boneless chicken breasts (8 ounces each)
2 tablespoons oil or enough oil for deep-frying
1-ounce package rice noodles
12 won ton wrappers, cut into strips and deep-fried
1 medium head iceburg lettuce, shredded
10 cilantro sprigs, coarsely chopped
2 cups finely chopped napa cabbage or won bok
1 cup bean sprouts
1 cup julienned red bell pepper
1 yellow bell pepper, julienned
1/2 cup thinly sliced (diagonally) green onions
1 medium carrot, grated
6 radishes, thinly sliced
1 cup whole macadamia nuts
4 whole cilantro sprigs, for garnish
1 head leaf lettuce, divided into leaves, for salad bed

MARINADE FOR CHICKEN

1 cup soy sauce
1 cup oil
4 tablespoons mirin
1 teaspoon sesame oil
4 tablespoons minced cilantro
2 tablespoons minced garlic
2 tablespoons minced ginger
1 teaspoon salt
1/2 teaspoon white pepper

2 tablespoons thinly sliced green onions
4 tablespoons cornstarch
3 teaspoons brown sugar

🔊 Combine and blend all marinade ingredients, except for cornstarch and brown sugar, which you will first mix together then add to marinade ingredients. Add chicken and marinate for 1 to 2 hours in the fridge.

🔊 Heat oil to 350°F. Drop rice noodles in oil and remove as soon as they puff up. (Don't brown them.) Drain on paper towels and break into bite-size pieces when cool. Set aside.

🔊 Cut won ton wrappers into strips and deep-fry until golden brown in same oil you used for the rice noodles. Drain on paper towels and set aside.

🔊 As soon as everything else is done and iceberg lettuce and other vegetables are sliced, chopped, and refrigerated, you can cook the chicken. Fry in 2 tablespoons oil, with skin on, until golden brown. Start on high heat, then finish on medium. After you turn the heat down, you can baste chicken with marinade. Continue basting, using about 1/2 cup of marinade in all, until liquid is absorbed and chicken is nicely browned. When done, let cool to room temperature and cut into strips.

🔊 Toss lettuce, cabbage, bean sprouts, and vegetables together with chicken and bite-size pieces of rice noodles in mixing bowl. Add half of macadamia nuts and half of fried won ton strips, and toss with salad, reserving remaining nuts and won ton strips for garnish.

🔊 Arrange on individual salad plates on a bed of your favorite leaf lettuce. Use 1/4 of remaining macadamia nuts, 1/4 of remaining fried won ton strips, and sprig of cilantro to garnish each salad.

🔊 Serve with your choice of dressing. I especially like the Traditional Sweet and Sour Vinaigrette with Cucumbers with this particular salad.

Chicken Avocado and Papaya Salad

Fresh ginger gives the wok-simmered chicken breasts a special zing. If you have time to make your own broth, great! If not, the low-sodium variety off the shelf works as well. My Creamy Oriental Dressing can be improved only by the sprinkle of macadamia nuts.

3/4 cup of Sam Choy's Creamy Oriental Dressing (see Note)
3 cups chicken stock or low-sodium chicken broth
1 thumb-size piece fresh ginger, peeled
3 whole skinless, boneless chicken breasts
2 ripe papayas, peeled, seeded and thinly sliced
2 ripe avocados, peeled, pitted and thinly sliced
salt and pepper to taste
1/3 cup diced macadamia nuts

ℬ Place 3 cups chicken stock in a wok and add fresh ginger. Bring the liquid to a boil and then add chicken breasts. Simmer for 15 minutes. Remove chicken breasts from liquid and refrigerate for 1 hour.

ℬ Cut chicken into thin slices. On individual salad plates, alternate slices of papaya, chicken and avocado. Spoon 2 tablespoons Sam's Creamy Oriental Dressing on each salad, then sprinkle with macadamia nuts.

NOTE: Either prepare Sam Choy's Creamy Oriental Dressing or purchase this dressing already bottled.

Beef Noodle Salad
with Peanuts

Taste as you add in the chili, peppers, garlic and cilantro. Make it full of flavor, not full of fire.

1 pound beef round tip
6-1/2 ounces dry cellophane noodles
1 tablespoon chili oil
1 teaspoon peeled and chopped garlic
1 cup shredded snow peas
1 tablespoon seeded and sliced hot red peppers
3 tablespoons soy sauce
2 tablespoons sweet chili sauce
1/4 cup chopped fresh cilantro leaves
1/3 cup roughly chopped, roasted unsalted peanuts
1 lime, cut into 6 wedges

🔊 Slice beef into strips, first cutting across the grain and then with the grain.

🔊 Place cellophane noodles in a medium-size bowl and cover with boiling water. Allow to stand for 4 minutes, or until soft; drain. Set aside.

🔊 Heat wok to high. Add chili oil and garlic and stir for 30 seconds. Add beef and stir-fry for 3 minutes, or until seared. Add snow peas and hot peppers and stir-fry for 2 minutes.

🔊 Mix soy sauce and sweet chili together and add to beef mixture. Stir briefly and remove from heat.

🔊 Toss stir-fry with cellophane noodles, cilantro leaves and chopped peanuts. Place on a serving platter and serve with wedges of lime.

Cover foods before and after serving so that bugs are not on the menu. Steamer trays are easy to rent and can be used with heat, as well as filled with ice. With an Island-style potluck, you can end up with the United Nations of foods. The more the merrier!

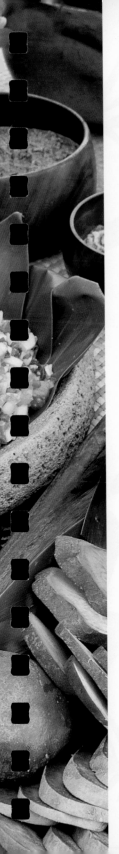

Side Dishes

*S*ide dishes are where the "melting pot" flavors really mix it up. Take a little Tahitian, throw in some Chinese, maybe some Filipino, Japanese, Korean or Portuguese-style recipes, and the result is guaranteed 'ono!

On the long serving table, place the side dishes between the salads and the entrée platters. Title cards, here and all along the table, label the dish and, if the party is potluck-style, the chef.

Side dishes are on your menu to enhance the entrée with multiple flavors. Plan the portions to be fairly small if you have several choices, but don't skimp. If Garlic Mashed Potatoes is someone's favorite, you'll need the extra!

Hibachi Mixed Vegetables

The variety of colors in this side dish makes it pretty for the plate. The secret here is the 30-minute multispiced marinade. Once these tasty vegetables come off the hibachi they won't be on the plate for long.

Mixed Vegetable Marinade (see recipe below)
2 cups oval sliced zucchini
2 cups oval sliced yellow squash
1 cup sliced red bell pepper
8 fresh shiitake mushrooms, rinsed and quartered

&) Mix sliced vegetables with marinade for 30 minutes.

&) Prepare coals for hibachi or barbecue grill. Cook vegetables over hibachi until done.

NOTE: To prevent vegetables from falling into the coals, use a grid or grilling mesh. This will make barbecuing small items like vegetables and fish a lot easier.

MIXED VEGETABLE MARINADE
Makes 1/3 Cup

1 teaspoon chopped fresh garlic
1/4 teaspoon black pepper
1/4 teaspoon chili sauce
1 teaspoon chopped fresh cilantro
1 teaspoon thyme leaves
1 tablespoon white wine
1 tablespoon salad oil
1 teaspoon sesame oil
1/4 teaspoon soy sauce
1/4 teaspoon oyster sauce

Baked Coconut Taro

This side dish combines the most basic of Polynesian flavors, coconut and taro, and goes well with any seafood dish. It's also one of the easiest ways to add authentic Island-style starch to your meal.

In Hawai'i taro has been the staple from earliest times to the present, and its culture developed to include more than 300 types. The entire plant is eaten, from its starchy root (often mashed into poi) to its heart-shaped leaves (known as lū'au).

1 pound fresh taro root, blanched and cubed
1/4 cup butter
1/4 cup coconut syrup
salt and white pepper to taste

GARNISH

coconut flakes, toasted
macadamia nuts, roasted and chopped

&ε Combine taro, butter, coconut, salt, and pepper in a covered casserole dish, and bake in 350°F oven for 35 minutes.

&ε To serve, garnish with toasted coconut and chopped roasted macadamia nuts.

Lomilomi Salmon
with a Twist

When you bite into the fried 'ōpae (shrimp), it's really good, sweet—plus the ogo. This is lomilomi salmon with something to chew on.

1 pound salted salmon (brine salmon)
1 cup dried shrimp
vegetable oil for deep-frying, such as safflower, cottonseed or corn oil
2 onions, diced
3 ripe medium-size tomatoes, diced
1/2 cup diced green onion
2 cups chopped fresh ogo (edible seaweed)

℞ Soak salmon in fresh water overnight in the refrigerator. Just before assembling salad, deep-fry dried shrimp. Heat oil to 350°F to 365°F. Use a deep-frying basket, if available. Fry shrimp just a few moments or until crunchy; drain on paper towel to remove extra oil.

℞ Rinse off excess salt from soaked salmon, discard skin and bones, and dice into small chunks. In a mixing bowl, combine all ingredients and don't forget "Sam Choy's twist"—the crunchy 'ōpae shrimp and the ogo. Chill until served.

Sweet Potato Casserole

My classmate Norman Masuto would give me the real big, off-grade sweet potatoes that his family grew in Kahuku. Top them off with brown sugar and sprinkle nuts on 'em if you want to.

6 to 8 medium sweet potatoes
3/4 cup packed brown sugar
1-1/4 cups butter
1 can (1 pound) crushed pineapple
1/2 cup coconut milk

🍠 Place sweet potatoes with their jackets in a steamer basket in 1-1/2 inches of boiling water. Steam covered for 25 minutes, or until tender. Peel and cut in 3/8-inch-thick slices. In a buttered casserole dish, layer half EACH of the sweet-potato slices, brown sugar, butter (dot with thin pats) and pineapple. Repeat layers. Pour coconut milk over all. Bake for 20 to 25 minutes at 350°F.

Garlic Mashed Potatoes

Makes 4 Servings

If you love garlic, you will absolutely want to share these potatoes with everyone.

4 to 5 medium sweet potatoes
2-1/4 pounds potatoes
4 whole cloves garlic
1/2 pound butter
3 ounces cream
white pepper and salt to taste

🍠 Peel and cut potatoes into 1-inch cubes. In a pot, cover potatoes with cold water, add garlic and bring to a boil. Cook for 8 to 10 minutes, or until done. Drain. Purée in a food processor, or whip with an electric mixer. Add the butter and cream. Season with salt and white pepper. Serve immediately.

Shiitake Mushroom Rice
with Shredded Ono Stir-Fry and Fresh Spinach

Using a delicate, delicious fish like ono creates a balance between the mushroom and spinach flavors. Add the jewel of rice, Basmati, and it's "'ono" all the way around.

1 ono (wahoo) fillet, cut diagonally into thin strips
2 teaspoons light olive oil
1 small onion, julienned
1/2 cup rinsed and sliced fresh shiitake mushrooms
1 teaspoon minced fresh garlic
2 teaspoons peeled and minced fresh ginger
1/4 cup chicken stock or low-sodium chicken broth
2 tablespoons oyster sauce
1/2 pound fresh spinach, washed and torn
salt and pepper to taste
3 cups cooked Basmati rice

GARNISH

straw mushrooms

๛ Cut ono into strips and prepare vegetables. Set aside.

๛ Heat a large wok and coat with oil. Stir-fry onion, shiitake mushrooms, garlic, and ginger for 1 minute. Add ono, and cook for 30 seconds, stirring constantly. Add chicken stock and oyster sauce. Cook for 1 minute.

๛ Add spinach, cooking until wilted. Add salt and pepper to taste. Add cooked Basmati rice and toss. Cover for 1 minute.

๛ To serve, garnish with straw mushrooms.

Sauces

My rule about sauces and dressings is that they should be good enough to eat with a spoon. Every sauce has a "best use," but that shouldn't stop you from trying my Creamy Oriental Dressing on chicken, vegetables or even a drizzle on bread. Name cards are not optional for the sauce dishes. You don't want someone smothering his teri-ribs with Sweet and Sour Sauce unless he actually likes it that way.

Here's my tip on sauce. Mix it up and try it out on something small before you cook ribs or make salad for thirty. See if the mix of flavors in the teri sauce is really pleasing to your pallet. Make changes. Add a spice. Make it your own. Then, when you love it, just remember to make some notes so you can do it again the next time!

Puna Papaya and Maui Onion Dressing

Makes About 3 Cups

1-1/2 small papayas, seeded and peeled
1/2 small Maui onion
1/4 cup rice vinegar, available in Asian section of supermarkets and in Asian markets
1 tablespoon sugar
1 cup canola oil
salt and pepper to taste

• Machine-process papaya, Maui onion, rice vinegar and sugar. With food processor or blender running, add oil in a slow, steady stream. Season with salt and pepper to taste.

Dill Vinaigrette

Make 1-1/4 Cups

1/4 cup rice vinegar, available in Asian section of markets
1/4 cup fresh dill
2 tablespoons sugar
1-1/2 tablespoons Maui onion diced
2 garlic cloves
salt and white pepper to taste
3/4 cup olive oil

• Machine-process all ingredients except oil. With food processor or blender running, add oil in a slow, steady stream.

Traditional Sweet-
and-Sour Vinaigrette
with Cucumbers

1 cup sugar
1/2 cup vinegar
1 cup pineapple juice
1/2 teaspoon salt
1-1/2 cups paper-thin sliced cucumber (one whole
    medium cucumber)
1 tablespoon minced fresh ginger
1/2 cup chopped macadamia nuts
fresh Hawaiian hot chili peppers or dried red pepper
    flakes, to taste

∞ Combine sugar, vinegar, pineapple juice, and salt and whisk real
well until everything is dissolved. Add the thinly sliced cucumber,
ginger, mac nuts, and chili peppers. Give it a stir, and taste.

Papaya-Mango Salsa

3 tablespoons sugar
1-1/2 tablespoons vinegar
pinch red chili pepper flakes
pinch cumin
1 medium peeled, seeded, and diced papaya
1 cup peeled and diced mango
1/2 small red onion, diced
3 tablespoons diced red bell pepper
2 tablespoons chopped cilantro

∞ Mix sugar, vinegar, chili flakes and cumin until sugar dissolves.
Fold in remaining ingredients.

Sam Choy's Creamy Oriental Dressing

I invented this to go on a hundred dishes. It is easy and quick. What's even quicker? Pick up my bottled version in the super-market!

3 cups mayonnaise
1/2 cup soy sauce
3/4 cup granulated sugar
1/4 teaspoon white pepper
1-1/2 tablespoons black sesame seeds
1 tablespoon sesame oil

೩ Place all ingredients in a medium-size bowl and whisk together until well blended. If necessary, whisk in a few drops of water at a time until you get the consistency you want. Refrigerate until used.

Balsamic Wasabi Vinaigrette

Makes 1 Cup

1 tablespoon wasabi paste
3/4 cup salad oil
1/4 cup balsamic vinegar
1/4 cup granulated sugar
1 teaspoon minced fresh garlic

೩ Combine ingredients and whisk together until well blended and sugar is dissolved. Refrigerate until used.

Wasabi Vinaigrette

2 cups orange juice (freshly squeezed is best)
3 tablespoons vinegar
1/2 cup oil
3 tablespoons sugar
2 tablespoons soy sauce
1 tablespoon salt
2 tablespoons sesame seeds
2 tablespoons wasabi

 Mix all ingredients together and blend well. Wasabi is Japanese horseradish that can be found in most supermarket Asian sections. If you like hot food, you might want to add more than I've suggested here, or less, if you prefer a milder flavor. Wasabi comes in either powder or paste form. If you buy the powder, you can make it into paste by adding a little water.

 A trick I learned from the Japanese is to make the paste with warm water if you want the wasabi really hot, then turn the mixing bowl with the paste in it upside down for about 3 minutes. This causes some sort of chemical reaction that brings out the fire.

Wasabi Mayonnaise

1 tablespoon wasabi powder
2 tablespoons water
1/2 cup mayonnaise
salt and pepper to taste

 Make a paste of the wasabi powder and water. Whisk into mayonnaise until completely mixed. Season with a pinch of salt and black pepper. Refrigerate.

My favorite lūʻau foods include the pig, lomilomi salmon, laulau, squid lūʻau, chicken long rice, sweet potatoes, poke, poi, lots of steamed rice, and, for dessert—haupia coconut squares, kulolo taro pudding, Kona cake, and Pineapple Upsidedown Cake. You can add in pūpū of all kinds, salads, fish and shellfish, side dishes, even soups. Just about anything works at a Backyard Lūʻau Party. Remember to keep things cold that should be cold and keep hot foods hot.

Fish

*I*f cooking fish isn't your strong point, do some trial runs. Begin with mahimahi. You can actually overcook this fish and it will still be moist. Most fish are very delicate and can be easily overcooked. Remember, even when you remove them from the heat, they continue to cook.

The recipes in this section are well suited to lūʻau-style serving. My best secret for fish: Buy fresh! Get to know the folks at the fish market. Tell them what dish you are preparing and take their suggestions—they're the experts. Remember, use a delicate hand with the seasonings. Don't let the sauce steal the show.

Grilled Marinated Mahimahi
with Pohā, Mango, and Papaya Relish

I like to start the coals going, then make the Pohā, Mango, and Papaya Relish, and put it in the refrigerator. Then comes the marinade, and we're on our way. This is a very easy, very elegant dish that tastes wonderful.

🔊 Marinate mahimahi for 10 minutes. Grill over medium coals for 2 to 3 minutes on each side. Remove from heat, and place on a platter over organic greens. Serve with Pohā, Mango, and Papaya Relish on the side.

MAHIMAHI MARINADE

1/2 cup crushed macadamia nuts
1/2 cup soy sauce
2 tablespoons honey
1/4 cup granulated sugar

🔊 Mix ingredients together until sugar is dissolved. Set aside.

POHĀ, MANGO, AND PAPAYA RELISH

1/2 cup medium-diced mango
1/4 cup medium-diced papaya
1/4 cup pohā berries, cut in half
1/4 cup small-diced red pepper
2 tablespoons small-diced yellow onions
2 tablespoons minced cilantro
1 tablespoon lime juice
2 tablespoons granulated sugar

🔊 Mix all ingredients together, and chill for 1 hour before serving.

Spicy Grilled Opah

Opah, or moonfish, has a sweet flavor that blends well with the spices used in this marinade and in the fruit chutney. Serve it up nice and hot with a couple scoops of rice. It's unreal.

Opah is one of the most colorful commercial fish species available in Hawai'i. A silvery-gray upper body shades to a rose red, dotted with white spots toward the belly. The fins of the opah are crimson, and its large eyes are encircled with gold. It's definitely a jewel of the ocean.

4 opah, 6-ounce fillets
Pineapple Chutney (see recipe on following page)

MARINADE

1/4 cup tomato juice
2 tablespoons fresh lemon juice
1 tablespoon dry sherry wine
2 tablespoons soy sauce
2 tablespoons brown sugar
1 tablespoon light olive oil
1 tablespoon minced fresh ginger
1/2 teaspoon ground cinnamon
1/2 teaspoon crushed anise seed
1/4 teaspoon ground nutmeg
1/4 teaspoon ground cloves
1 teaspoon sambal oelek (chili paste)
salt to taste

🔊 Mix marinade ingredients in shallow glass or plastic dish. Add fish; turn to coat with marinade. Cover, and refrigerate for 1 hour.

🔊 Remove fish from marinade; reserve marinade. Cover, and grill fish for 10 to 15 minutes, about 4 inches from medium-high coals. Brush occasionally with marinade, and turn once.

🔊 Serve with Pineapple Chutney.

PINEAPPLE CHUTNEY

2 cups chopped fresh pineapple
1 cup raisins
1 tablespoon finely chopped fresh ginger
1 tablespoon finely chopped fresh garlic
1/2 tablespoon sambal oelek (chili paste)
1/2 cup rice vinegar
3/4 cup brown sugar
1/2 teaspoon ground cinnamon
1/2 teaspoon salt
1/2 cup chopped macadamia nuts

ɞ Combine everything (except nuts) in a large saucepan, and cook slowly until pineapple is tender, about 30 minutes. Stir in nuts, and cook until chutney is of desired consistency. Makes about 1 quart.

Sautéed 'Ōpakapaka
with Spinach Coconut Lū'au Sauce

Makes 4 Servings

Here's a takeoff on squid lū'au. Take out the squid from that recipe, make a thinner sauce and add it to 'ōpakapaka, an excellent flaky fish. The combination is just right—really, really 'ono.

4 'ōpakapaka (pink snapper) fillets (6 ounces each)
1 teaspoon minced fresh ginger
1 teaspoon minced garlic
1/2 teaspoon salt
1/4 teaspoon white pepper
1/4 cup flour
2 tablespoons butter
1 tablespoon olive oil
Spinach Coconut Lū'au Sauce (see recipe on
    following page)

ɞ Season 'ōpakapaka fillets with ginger, garlic, salt and pepper. Dredge in flour. In a large heavy skillet, heat butter and oil. Sauté fish until just cooked; do not overcook.

⊗ Transfer fish to a warm serving platter and serve with Spinach Coconut Lū'au Sauce.

SPINACH COCONUT LŪ'AU SAUCE
Makes 10 (1-Ounce) Servings

3 tablespoons minced Maui onion
1/2 tablespoon minced fresh ginger
2 tablespoons butter
1 cup heavy cream
1/4 cup coconut milk
salt, pepper and sugar to taste
1/2 cup cooked fresh lū'au (young taro leaves; chopped
  fresh spinach can be used as a substitute)

⊗ In a small saucepan, sauté onion and ginger in butter for 3 minutes, or until onion is translucent. Add heavy cream, bring to a boil and reduce by half. Stir in cooked lū'au (or spinach) and coconut milk, and cook for 2 minutes. Season to taste with salt, pepper, and sugar.

'Ahi with Lime-Shoyu Marinade
Makes 4 Servings

The lime juice in the "Lime-Shoyu Marinade" will "acid cook" the 'ahi fillets. It will also seal in the 'ahi juices, making the finished, grilled fish succulent and moist. I still caution to not overcook your fish.

'Ahi, like all fish, tends to dry out when cooked too long. To avoid turning a beautiful fillet into a tough chunk of meat, I marinate the fish, then cook it rather quickly. That way I lock in the flavors and the fish's natural juices. I know I say it all the time, but DO NOT OVERCOOK your fish.

4 'ahi (yellowfin tuna) fillets (6 ounces each)

LIME-SHOYU MARINADE

1/4 cup soy sauce
1/4 cup oil
juice and grated zest of 1 lime
2 tablespoons dry sherry
2 tablespoons chopped cilantro
1 tablespoon minced fresh garlic
1 tablespoon brown sugar
2 teaspoons minced fresh ginger
1/8 teaspoon Chinese 5-Spice Powder

ⅆ Combine marinade ingredients, and marinate fish for 30 minutes, turning occasionally. Grill or broil fish for 5 to 6 minutes on each side, basting with marinade.

ⅆ Do not overcook.

Poached Salmon
with Tropical Fruit Salsa

Makes 4 Servings

Seasoning is important, but you have to make sure you don't overseason. Most of my recipes call for salt and pepper to taste, but even if I forget to mention it here or there, you should still do it. I am known for blending small amounts of various spices in interesting ways so that the season enhances rather than overpowers the food. I never use MSG—it's not necessary. The proper use of seasoning is to guide the natural flavors and bring out the best. For example, a little sugar added to something salty doesn't make it taste sweet, it just brings the flavor to a peak and rounds it out. Fresh herbs make a big difference and should always be added at the end of cooking, as their flavor evaporates if cooked too long. We're lucky in Hawai'i to have various fresh fruits throughout the year, and those flavors, combined with the distinct taste of salmon, makes for a very interesting dish.

3 salmon fillets (3 ounces each)
sprigs of fresh herbs for garnish

POACHING WATER

4 cups water
1/2 cup chopped cilantro
2 cups white wine
1 cup mixture of diced carrots, onions, and celery
juice of 1 lemon
1 teaspoon salt
1/2 teaspoon cracked pepper

TROPICAL FRUIT SALSA

1 cup diced mangoes or lychee, or seasonal tropical fruit
1 cup diced papaya
1 cup diced pineapple
1/2 cup cilantro
1/4 cup diced red bell pepper
1/4 cup diced tomatoes
salt and pepper to taste
1 teaspoon cumin
1/2 teaspoon hot red pepper flakes

ⅎ Blend together all salsa ingredients and let sit at room temperature for 30 minutes.

ⅎ Mix poaching water ingredients and bring water to a boil. Poach salmon about 3 to 4 minutes, depending on thickness of fillets. As soon as salmon turns opaque in the middle, it's done. Myself, I like to leave the fish a little raw in the middle—it seems to taste better.

ⅎ Divide the salsa into four portions. On each plate place a layer of salsa, two fish fillets, and a dollop of salsa on top of fish.

ⅎ Garnish with a sprig of the fresh herb of your choice.

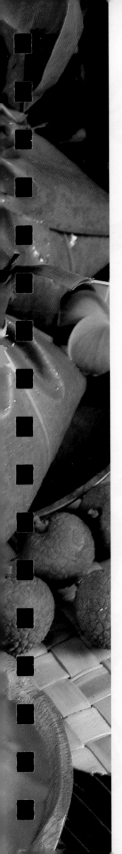

Chicken

Chicken may be the most creative lū'au food. It is so versatile that it could be its own entire cookbook. Cut off the skin and fat and you have a perfect protein. Handle it carefully. Wash it before use. Defrost in the refrigerator and never re-freeze. Cook it until there is no pink along the bone. Be safe. But remember, overcooked chicken can be like cardboard.

Chicken can take the spices. It almost calls out, "Bring it on." Have some fun with flavors. Try out some new spices. Since it cooks quickly, you can do several "taste tests" in advance of your big party. If you happen to roast too much, you can always chop it and save it for the Chicken Salad.

Hibachi Miso Chicken
with Peanut Butter

The marinade melds traditional and modern flavors—miso and teriyaki with peanut butter and beer. Kamado-grill or cover-grill (Weber enclosed grill) the fillets for 35 minutes, or skewer and grill.

5 pounds boneless chicken thighs

MARINADE

1/2 cup miso (fermented soybean paste), available in Asian sections of markets
1/2 cup creamy peanut butter
1/2 cup soy sauce
1/2 cup sugar
1/2 cup beer
2 tablespoons minced fresh ginger
1 tablespoon minced garlic

ɛɔ Combine marinade ingredients and marinate chicken overnight in refrigerator. Grill over charcoal. There is not enough rice in the world to eat when you start eating this dish!

Chicken and Portuguese Sausage Kabobs

Makes 8 Servings

This is an alternative fund-raiser dish. I got the kabob idea as an alternative for those 10 or 15 packages of Portuguese sausage the kids sell to raise funds during baseball season.

1 pound skinless, boneless chicken breast, cut in 1-inch cubes
1 Portuguese sausage (1 pound), cut in 1-inch chunks
24 fresh pineapple wedges

MARINADE

1 cup dry red wine
1/2 cup olive oil
1/4 cup red wine vinegar
1/4 cup orange juice
2 tablespoons pineapple juice
3 large cloves garlic, minced
1 tablespoon chopped fresh basil
salt and cracked peppercorn to taste

&) Whisk marinade ingredients together well and marinate chicken cubes for 2 or 3 hours. Drain chicken and reserve marinade. On skewers, alternately thread meats and fruit; leave space between chicken and sausage to allow for even cooking. Grill over medium-hot coals for 12 minutes, or until chicken and sausage are cooked, basting frequently with reserved marinade.

Chicken and Coconut Milk

Makes 6 Servings

Canned spinach can be used, along with canned coconut milk. The chicken can be anything, as long as it is boneless. This is a quick Hawaiian favorite that can look as if you cooked all day.

2 pounds boneless, skinless chicken
2 cups coconut milk
2 cups steamed spinach (see Note)
salt to taste
1 quart low-sodium chicken broth

&) Cut chicken into 2-inch pieces, place in a pot and cover with chicken broth. Simmer over low heat for 10 to 15 minutes. Add coconut milk and cook for 30 minutes, or until tender. Add the cooked and drained spinach; salt to taste and simmer for 5 minutes.

NOTE: 2 cups canned or frozen spinach can be used in place of 2 cups steamed fresh spinach.

By using chicken breast, a low-fat coconut milk, a lower fat, low-sodium chicken broth, you can minimize fat without compromising flavor.

Quick and Easy Shoyu Chicken

Shoyu chicken, an island classic, features gourmet touches of cilantro, Chinese five spices and fresh-squeezed orange juice.

1 tablespoon minced cilantro
1/2 teaspoon Chinese five-spice powder, available in
  supermarkets
2 pounds chicken thighs
1 tablespoon cornstarch
2 tablespoons water
green onions
bean sprouts
Tailgate Teri Sauce (see recipe below)

୨୦ In a medium saucepan, combine Tailgate Teri Sauce, cilantro and Chinese five-spice powder. Bring to a boil, add chicken, then simmer for 20 minutes, or until tender. Remove chicken from sauce, set aside and keep warm.

୨୦ Blend cornstarch and water to make a smooth paste. Bring 1 cup of sauce to a boil and stir in cornstarch paste to thicken into a glaze. Brush chicken with glaze. Garnish with green onions and bean sprouts.

TAILGATE TERI SAUCE

1 cup soy sauce
juice from 1 medium orange
1/2 cup mirin
1/2 cup water
1/4 cup brown sugar
1-1/2 teaspoons minced garlic
1-1/2 teaspoons minced ginger

୨୦ Combine all ingredients and mix well.

Sweet-and-Sour Chicken Breasts
with Tropical Fruits

Makes 4 Servings

I really like doing this dish because it gives you a whole new twist on cooking, beyond the basic sweet-and-sour sauce. Adding the fresh tropical fruits really makes it good, and different. It takes away the boredom.

4 chicken breasts (6 to 8 ounces each)
1-1/2 cups flour
3 tablespoons oil
1 cup diced fresh pineapple
1 cup chopped fresh papaya
1 cup chopped mangoes, or tropical fruit of your choice

MARINADE

1/2 cup soy sauce
1/2 cup oil
2 tablespoons mirin
1 tablespoon minced garlic
1 tablespoon minced ginger
1/2 teaspoon salt
1/4 teaspoon white pepper
2 tablespoons cornstarch
1-1/2 teaspoons brown sugar

SWEET-AND-SOUR SAUCE

1/2 cup tomato catsup
1/2 cup vinegar
1/2 cup water
2 teaspoons soy sauce
1 cup sugar
1/4 cup orange marmalade
1-1/2 teaspoons minced ginger
1 teaspoon minced garlic
1/4 teaspoon hot pepper sauce

2 tablespoons pineapple juice
2 tablespoons cornstarch blended with 1-1/2 tablespoons
  water

GARNISH

green onion strips
sprigs of fresh cilantro

❧ Combine marinade ingredients and marinate chicken for 30 minutes.

❧ Make Sweet-and-Sour Sauce by combining all ingredients, except cornstarch mixture, in a medium saucepan. Bring to a boil. Add cornstarch mixture, reduce heat and simmer, stirring frequently, until thickened.

❧ Blot excess liquid off chicken and dust with flour to coat. Pan-fry in 3 tablespoons oil until golden brown, about 4 minutes per side on medium heat. Remove chicken, set aside, and keep warm.

❧ Discard excess oil in pan, leaving about 1 tablespoon. Stir-fry fruit in oil for 2 minutes. Add Sweet-and-Sour sauce and heat through.

❧ Arrange chicken breasts on serving platter, pour sauce over chicken and garnish with green onions and cilantro.

Curried Citrus Papaya Chicken

Makes 8 Servings

You can't beat fruit with chicken, especially the blended flavors of papaya, citrus, and curry. The frying is quick, then you can relax while the rice cooks and the Curried Citrus Sauce bakes into the boneless chicken meat.

Curried Citrus Sauce (see recipe on following page)
3 pounds skinless, boneless chicken thighs
1 cup all-purpose flour

2 teaspoons curry powder
1 teaspoon paprika
1 teaspoon salt
1 teaspoon white pepper
2 tablespoons salad oil
2 teaspoons peeled and minced ginger
2 teaspoons minced fresh garlic
2 teaspoons fresh cilantro

GARNISH

sliced papaya and citrus fruits
cilantro

🔊 Preheat oven to 350°F.

🔊 Combine flour, curry powder, paprika, salt and white pepper in a large bowl. Dredge chicken in flour mixture and shake off excess. In a large skillet or wok, coat the bottom with salad oil. Pan-fry chicken until golden brown. Place fried chicken in a baking pan, pour Curried Citrus Sauce over the top of the chicken and sprinkle ginger, garlic and cilantro on top. Bake for 45 minutes. Place on top of a bed of rice and garnish with sliced fruit and cilantro.

NOTE: In place of chicken thigh, use skinless, boneless chicken breast to reduce the fat.

CURRIED CITRUS SAUCE

Makes 1-1/2 Cups

1-1/2 cups orange juice
2 teaspoons curry powder
1 tablespoon cornstarch
1/3 cup brown sugar
2 cups sliced papaya

🔊 Mix ingredients together until sugar is dissolved.

Chicken

Don't let the idea of a lū'au worry you. Jump in. Hey, it's one way to get really close to your friends and family. No telling how many planning and work gatherings will turn into full-on parties before you even get to the big day. Good food, good friends—it just doesn't get any better than that! Now, enjoy!

Shellfish

Shellfish work well on a barbecue grill or over open coals. You can enlist the assistance of a guest or two, asking them to turn the shrimp on the barbecue. When one round is done, change guest-chefs and add a new shellfish. Even if your lūʻau is indoors, you can put someone in charge of cooking on the small hibachi on the lānai.

If you are using shellfish with the shells on, make sure you wash them well. Sand in the teeth takes the glow off the dining experience! Remember, shellfish cook quickly. Watch the fire and scoop them off before you have rubber! Keep in mind that they have delicate flavors. Your seasoning can be innovative, just not overpowering.

Tequila-Grilled Shrimp

This is a real "tropical-looking" dish. It's a mellow "make you smile" treat.

1 pound jumbo shrimp, peeled and deveined

MARINADE

1/4 cup corn oil
1/4 cup tequila
1/4 cup red wine vinegar
2 tablespoons fresh lime juice
1/2 teaspoon salt
1 tablespoon chili garlic sauce
1 red bell pepper, diced
1 clove fresh garlic, minced
1/3 cup minced onion
1/4 cup minced fresh cilantro

GARNISH

papaya, mango, cilantro, chopped

🔊 Mix marinade ingredients in a shallow glass or plastic dish. Add shrimp, cover, and refrigerate for 1 hour.

🔊 Remove shrimp from marinade; reserve marinade. Thread six shrimp on each of six 8-inch metal skewers. Grill over medium coals, turning once, until pink, 2 to 3 minutes on each side.

🔊 Bring marinade to a boil in non-aluminum (or non-reactive) saucepan; reduce heat to low. Simmer uncovered for about 5 minutes. Serve with shrimp.

TO BROIL

🔊 Set oven control to broil. Place skewered shrimp on rack in broiler pan. Broil with tops about 4 inches from heat, turning once, until pink, 2 or 3 minutes on each side.

🔊 Lay the shrimp skewers side-by-side on a serving platter, and scatter mango and papaya chunks over the top. Sprinkle with chopped cilantro.

Hilo Mango-Liliko'i-Basil Barbecue Shrimp

Mango has a flavor of its own. Liliko'i (passion fruit) blends with all that spicy marinated shrimp-on-a-skewer. Sprinkle basil on top...I'm getting hungry already!

1 pound shrimp (about 16 to 20)
2 large mangoes, each cut in 6 large chunks

MARINADE

1/2 cup mango purée
1/2 cup frozen liliko'i concentrate, thawed
1 tablespoon brown sugar
1 tablespoon minced fresh basil
1 tablespoon chopped fresh dill
1 teaspoon minced fresh ginger
1/2 teaspoon minced garlic

෨ Peel and devein shrimp, leaving tails on. Combine marinade ingredients and marinate shrimp for 1 hour.

෨ On each of four skewers, alternately thread shrimp and mango chunks. Grill or broil kabobs for 7 minutes, or until shrimp is cooked—turning once and basting occasionally with marinade.

Wok Barbecue Shrimp
with Pepper-Papaya-Pineapple Chutney

Fire up wok-cooked shellfish with the zesty flavors of fresh ginger and Asian and Hawaiian chilies.

1 pound extra-large shrimp (about 16 to 20)
1-1/2 tablespoons canola oil

MARINADE

1/4 cup canola oil
2 tablespoons soy sauce
2 tablespoons chopped cilantro
1 tablespoon minced garlic
1/2 teaspoon sugar
1 Hawaiian chili pepper, seeded and chopped
   (or 1/8 teaspoon red chili pepper flakes)
Pepper-Papaya-Pineapple Chutney (see recipe below)

🙳 To prepare shrimp, rinse and cut through shell along top of back, but not all the way through to the meat. Peel shell from shrimp, leaving shell and tail attached at tail. Devein.

🙳 Combine marinade ingredients and marinate shrimp for 30 minutes. In a wok, heat the 1-1/2 tablespoons oil and sauté marinated shrimp for 4 or 5 minutes. Do not overcook. Serve with Pepper-Papaya-Pineapple Chutney.

PEPPER-PAPAYA-PINEAPPLE CHUTNEY
Makes 1-1/2 Cups

1 small fresh pineapple, peeled, cored and chopped
1 medium fresh papaya, seeded, peeled and chopped
1 tablespoon minced fresh ginger
6 tablespoons sugar
1 tablespoon hot chili paste, such as Southeast Asian sambal

🙳 In a medium saucepan, combine all ingredients except chili paste. Cook on medium heat for 1 hour or until mixture has a syrupy consistency. Fold in chili paste.

Sautéed Scallops with Lū'au Sauce

Lū'au is the name for young taro tops. The name eventually became the name of a big Hawaiian feast. In this case, the scallops in lū'au sauce really is a feast. With the stems removed, you blanch the leaves. The sauce is creamy with coconut milk, butter and heavy cream. Add the lū'au leaves, simmer, plate and let the golden brown scallops float in the center.

Lū'au Sauce (see recipe below)
2 pounds fresh large scallops
2 tablespoons all-purpose flour
salt and pepper to taste
1 tablespoon salad oil

Rinse scallops in cold water and drain well on paper towels. Combine flour with salt and pepper. Dust scallops with flour mixture. Place oil in sauté pan and heat to medium-high. Sauté scallops until evenly browned.

Ladle Lū'au Sauce onto individual plates and arrange scallops on top. Serve.

LŪ'AU SAUCE
Makes 2 Cups

1 cup cooked and chopped lū'au leaves (young taro leaves), or spinach leaves
1/2 cup diced onions
2 tablespoons butter
1/4 cup heavy cream
1/4 cup coconut milk
salt and pepper to taste
1 tablespoon granulated sugar
1/2 cup chicken stock or low-sodium chicken broth

To cook lū'au leaves, remove stem from leaves, chop and then blanch in boiling water for 3 to 5 minutes. Strain in colander.

In a saucepan, brown onions in butter over medium heat. Add heavy cream and coconut milk. Season with salt, pepper, and sugar. Let simmer for 5 minutes. Add cooked lū'au leaves and chicken stock. Simmer for 15 to 20 minutes.

Broiled Lobster
with Basil-Garlic Butter Sauce and Grilled Corn Relish

Lobsters are great for barbecues because they come in their own self-contained package. Just throw them over the coals, cover the grill, and let them cook, or broil them in the oven. The meat stays quite moist, protected by the hard shell. They're traditionally served with butter, but adding a little basil is just the perfect touch to spice up the flavor.

Many local grocery stores have fish and meat sections that display live Maine lobsters swimming in tanks. These delicious hard-shelled creatures are categorized and priced in three sizes. Most weigh about 1-1/4 pounds, and each one is considered a single portion. Large lobsters weigh more than 1-1/2 pounds. And extra-large lobsters weigh 2-1/4 pounds or more.

1-1/2 pounds fresh, live Maine lobster
salt and pepper to taste
Basil-Garlic Butter Sauce (see recipe on following page)
Grilled Corn Relish (see recipe on following page)

GARNISH
lemon wedges

🔊 Cut lobster in half, season with salt and pepper, and broil until cooked.

🔊 To serve, place lobster on a platter, and drizzle with Basil-Garlic Butter Sauce, or serve Basil-Garlic Butter Sauce in ramekin dish on the side for dipping. Garnish lobster with lemon wedges, and serve with Grilled Corn Relish.

BASIL-GARLIC BUTTER SAUCE

6 tablespoons softened butter
2 teaspoons puréed fresh garlic
1 tablespoon minced fresh basil
juice of 1/2 fresh lemon
salt and pepper to taste

⁖ Heat butter, and add the rest of the ingredients, except basil. Cook until garlic is translucent. Add basil and cook for 30 seconds.

GRILLED CORN RELISH

1/2 onion, chopped
1/2 cup chopped red pepper
2 tablespoons light olive oil
1 teaspoon minced garlic
3 corn cobs, grilled, then shucked
salt and pepper to taste
1/4 cup coarsely chopped cilantro

⁖ Sauté the onions and pepper with olive oil. Add garlic and grilled corn kernels. Add salt and pepper to taste. Fold in cilantro.

Stuffed Calamari
with Apple Banana and Cooked on the Hibachi

Makes 4 Servings

One day, a neighbor brought over a handful of really tasty apple bananas from his yard. They were small and tart and really 'ono. I got some calamari from some fishermen in Kailua-Kona, and decided to stuff the calamari with the bananas. It turned out GREAT! Try it.

When grilling unskewered shellfish like shrimp and calamari, it's good to use a fine-meshed, well-oiled fish grate. It makes handling the smaller foods much easier. It lets the smoky flavor permeate the meat without allowing the fish to fall through the grill.

1 pound fresh calamari
1 tablespoon minced fresh garlic
1 tablespoon minced fresh ginger
1/2 tablespoon cracked peppercorn
1/2 teaspoon chopped fresh basil
3/4 cup mirin (Japanese sweet rice wine)
2 tablespoons soy sauce
2 tablespoons macadamia nut oil
1 teaspoon granulated sugar
1 tablespoon minced fresh cilantro
12 ripe apple bananas, split in half
Tropical Fruit Salsa (see recipe below)

&o Clean calamari. In a large mixing bowl, blend all of the ingredients together, and pour over calamari. Let marinate for 1 hour. Stuff calamari lengthwise with apple bananas, then lightly score sides to add elasticity during cooking. (Be careful not to pierce through the calamari skin.) Place on the hibachi to cook for about 3 minutes on each side. Serve with Tropical Fruit Salsa.

TROPICAL FRUIT SALSA

1/2 cup white wine vinegar
3 tablespoons granulated sugar
1/4 teaspoon ground cumin
1/2 cup chopped fresh cilantro
1 tablespoon minced fresh ginger
1/2 cup chopped mango
1/2 cup chopped pineapple
1/2 cup chopped papaya
1 red bell pepper, chopped
2 Hawaiian chili peppers, minced

&o Blend vinegar, sugar, cumin, cilantro, and ginger until sugar dissolves. Then fold into fruit and set aside.

Shellfish

Pork and Beef

Now, the pig. I have given you all the directions to dig the hole. If you are doing the "big one," just follow the step-by-step. If you opt for the simpler lūʻau, then the No-Imu Kālua Pig is the way to go. Add some grilled ribs or beef kabobs and it's a flavor fest!

This section contains some of my very favorite recipes for pork and beef on the barbecue. Some can go barbecue, oven, broiler or rotisserie. They all share one thing, flavor! You want the pork and beef dishes to be bold enough to be memorable. I like to rub the spices into the meat, lomilomi (massage) the marinade into the fibers. It's the loving touch that gives off the special flavor. Delicious! Remember, make plenty. There is something about eating outside that makes folks extra hungry!

Barbecue Beef Short Ribs

The rub-salt-on-ribs step may be critical. I like to massage spicing into meats and fish, feeling where and how a recipe will take me.

1 clove garlic, minced
sea salt and pepper to taste
4 pounds 3-bone beef short ribs

BARBECUE SAUCE

2 strips bacon, minced
1 tablespoon finely chopped onion
1 can (8 ounces) tomato sauce
1/4 cup orange juice
2 tablespoons rice vinegar
2 tablespoons brown sugar
1 tablespoon Worcestershire sauce
1 teaspoon red chili pepper flakes

&ℴ Rub garlic, sea salt and pepper on ribs and let stand while making barbecue sauce.

&ℴ In a sauté pan, brown bacon and onion. Add remaining barbecue sauce ingredients. Bring to a boil, reduce heat and simmer, stirring constantly, for 10 minutes.

&ℴ On an open grill, barbecue ribs while basting frequently with barbecue sauce to keep meat moist. Serve with grilled red potatoes.

Tailgate Teri Steaks

Makes 4 Servings

At one of the University of Hawai'i vs. Brigham Young-Provo football games, we had live lobsters, steaks and shrimp in the cooler. Pūlehu (barbecue) Tailgate Teriyaki on the hibachi; it's always good.

4 lean New York steaks (10 ounces each)
1 tablespoon cornstarch
1 tablespoon cold water
pineapple wedges
toasted coconut

TERIYAKI SAUCE

2 cups soy sauce
1 cup mirin
1 cup water
1/2 cup brown sugar
3 teaspoons minced garlic
3 teaspoons minced ginger

🔊 Combine Teriyaki Sauce ingredients and reserve 1 cup. In remaining 3 cups sauce, marinate steaks 4 to 6 hours, turning occasionally.

🔊 Blend cornstarch and water to make a paste. Bring reserved marinade to a boil and stir in cornstarch paste to thicken. Grill or broil steaks to desired doneness, basting with thickened sauce.

🔊 Grill or broil pineapple wedges. Garnish each steak with a broiled pineapple wedge and a sprinkling of toasted coconut.

Hulihuli (Rotisserie) Beef

Makes 10 to 16 Servings

It's very impressive when you go to a backyard party or a family gathering and see this massive side of beef turning over the coals, and you ask yourself how you can do it at home. That's why I've included this recipe, so you can do rotisserie beef yourself and have it look awesome and impressive, as well as have it taste real good.

**1 whole cross-rib roast (4 pounds), or bottom round, or tri-tip
4 cups sweet vermouth, for basting**

MARINADE

**1 tablespoon cracked peppercorns
sea salt, as needed
2 tablespoons minced garlic
2 tablespoons minced ginger**

🔊 Combine marinade ingredients, massage into roast, and let marinate for 15 minutes. Place roast on skewer and secure into rotisserie over hot coals. (Don't cover.)

🔊 Plan on about 2 hours of cooking time. Baste every 10 to 20 minutes with sweet vermouth, until the last 30 minutes. Then baste about every 5 minutes. If you don't have a rotisserie, it can be done in a closed outdoor barbecue system by turning the meat every half hour and basting in the same manner as for the rotisserie method.

Hoisin Pūlehu Pork Chops

Hoisin sauce has a tasty zing to it; goes great on pork.

4 lean pork rib chops (each 1-1/4 inches thick—
    2 pounds total)

MARINADE

3 tablespoons hoisin sauce (Chinese sweet-spicy soybean
    paste), available in supermarkets and Asian markets
1 tablespoon soy sauce
2 teaspoons orange juice
1 green onion, sliced
1 teaspoon minced fresh ginger
1 clove ginger, minced
1/8 teaspoon Chinese five-spice powder
dash ground pepper

🔊 Combine marinade ingredients and marinate pork chops for
1 hour. Grill 20 to 30 minutes, basting with marinade to keep meat
moist.

🔊 Do not overcook.

🔊 Serve with assorted grilled vegetables of choice.

COOKING TIP: Here's a little trick I do: I add citrus—freshly
squeezed orange juice or orange concentrate—to my marinades.
Slice an orange and squeeze the juice right in, just like for breakfast. I like using citrus because it has a really nice, mellow flavor.

Hawaiian Pūlehu Tri-Tip Steak

This is a big piece of beef, and what makes it really good is that it's crusty on the outside and nice and rare on the inside, almost like beef sashimi. It's great eating when it's hot, and it makes the best cold sandwiches the next day after the flavors have had a chance to be absorbed all through the meat.

2-1/2 pounds tri-tip steak (triangular tip of the sirloin)
1/2 cup sea salt
1 tablespoon minced fresh garlic
1/2 tablespoon cracked peppercorn
1 tablespoon granulated sugar

  Prepare your charcoal for grilling.

  Rub salt, garlic, pepper and sugar into the meat and let sit for 30 minutes. Pūlehu in Hawaiian means "to broil on hot embers" and that's what you do, turning the meat every 4 minutes until done. Total cooking time is about 10 to 15 minutes, depending on the thickness of the cut.

Sweet-and-Sour Pineapple Pork

This is a really local dish with heavy Asian influence, as well as a distinctive Hawaiian touch. Coming as I do from the hills of Wahiawā on Oʻahu's North Shore, I'd often drive past fields of pineapple and see all the pickers out there working, but I never gave it much thought until 1968, when I went to work for eight weeks in a Lānaʻi pineapple field. When you see the pickers out there working, it looks easy, but, man, it's really hard work.

1 pound lean pork
1 tablespoon soy sauce
1 tablespoon sweet vermouth
1 teaspoon minced garlic
1 teaspoon minced ginger
2 tablespoons oil
1/2 cup cornstarch
4 cups oil for deep-fat frying
2 tablespoons oil
1/2 cup diced red and yellow bell peppers
2 tablespoons diced onion
Sweet-and-Sour Sauce (see recipe below)
strips of green onion, for garnish
toasted sesame seeds, for garnish

SWEET-AND-SOUR SAUCE

1/2 cup tomato catsup
1/2 cup vinegar
1/2 cup water
2 teaspoons soy sauce
1 cup sugar
1/4 cup orange marmalade
1-1/2 teaspoons minced ginger
1 teaspoon minced garlic

A Hawaiian Lūʻau *with Sam Choy and the Mākaha Sons*   **134**

1/4 teaspoon hot pepper sauce
2 tablespoons pineapple juice
1/2 cup chopped canned pineapple
4 tablespoons cornstarch mixed with 3 tablespoons water,
  for thickening

℘ Cut pork into bite-size pieces and marinate for 30 minutes in mixture of soy sauce, vermouth, garlic, ginger, and 2 tablespoons oil. Set aside. Meanwhile, make the Sweet-and-Sour Sauce.

℘ In a medium saucepan, combine all Sweet-and-Sour Sauce ingredients except cornstarch mixture, blend well, and bring to a boil. Add cornstarch mixture. Reduce heat and simmer, stirring frequently, until thickened. Be sure and bring your sauce to a boil before adding the cornstarch, otherwise the sauce may retain an unpleasant starchy taste. (The amount of cornstarch in my recipes is just a suggestion; you may want to add more for a thicker sauce. But be careful. A little cornstarch goes a long way.)

℘ Remove pork pieces from marinade and roll in cornstarch to coat well. Deep fry in 330°F to 350°F oil until golden brown and crispy.

℘ In a large sauté pan, heat 2 tablespoons oil on medium-high heat. Stir-fry red and yellow bell peppers and diced onion for 2 minutes, then add Sweet-and-Sour Sauce and fold in fried pork. Let simmer for 2 minutes, arrange on serving platter and garnish with long strips of green onion and toasted sesame seeds.

℘ This is the first recipe my dad taught me to cook when I was 12 years old. Tastes great with steamed rice.

Hale'iwa Barbecue Pork Ribs

Cook this dish ahead of time, then pack up the family and the hibachi and head for the park. A quick reheat over the coals and the flavor becomes twice as good. Be sure to make a big batch. Just the effort of eating outside can make you twice as hungry!

Hale'iwa Barbecue Sauce (see recipe on following page)
2 whole slabs pork ribs, cut into sections of 3 ribs each
water to cover ribs in stockpot
1/2 cup sea salt
4 cloves garlic, whole
1 finger fresh ginger, whole
2 green onions, whole

೫ Place ribs in stockpot and cover with water. Start with 1/2 cup sea salt and keep adding until water tastes salty, then add garlic, ginger, and green onions. Bring to a boil. Reduce heat and let simmer for 45 to 60 minutes, or until ribs are tender. Remove ribs from stockpot and let cool.

೫ Heat hibachi until coals are hot. Brush ribs with barbecue sauce and grill until thoroughly heated. Baste the ribs with barbecue sauce as they cook.

HALE'IWA BARBECUE SAUCE

Makes About 8 Cups

1 teaspoon red chili flakes
2 cans (15 ounces each) tomato sauce
2 cups brown sugar
1/2 cup vinegar
1/2 cup honey
2 cups minced onion
2 teaspoons liquid smoke
2 teaspoons chili powder
1 teaspoon coarsely cracked black pepper
2 tablespoons steak sauce
1/2 teaspoon dry mustard
1 cinnamon stick
1 cup canned crushed pineapple
1 tablespoon minced fresh garlic

❧ Combine all barbecue sauce ingredients in a saucepan, bring to a boil, reduce heat and simmer for 1 hour. Strain.

Pork and Beef

Even if there is a big crowd and a full-on imu involved, most family-planned Hawaiian lūʻau take on the feel of a backyard party. That is the best part of having a lūʻau. It can feel much like a big family picnic in the South or the Midwest. Only thing is, horseshoes and baseball may replace surfing and beach volleyball after the meal.

Desserts

My wife is the dessert maker of our family. She tells me that baking is not like cooking. You can't throw in a little of this and a little of that. It is a science, she says.

Hawai'i has many unbelievable dessert flavors. The fruits and macadamia nuts, mixed as sorbets and sauces or combined with coconut milk—ummmm!

Just a platter of fresh fruits is luscious enough. Here I've included an assortment of my favorites. You can use the same trick with the "chill" box of ice to keep the coconut and haupia dishes cool. Sorbets and frozen desserts need big coolers with lots of blue ice or a freezer very close by. The Banana Poi—Tahitian-Style with Haupia Ice Cream is a dish you may feel the need to test several times! 'Onolicious!

Grilled Tropical Fruits

Pre-pack an array of enticing fruits for a picnic, then caramelize the fruits over a hibachi. Another of brother Patrick's wonders.

1 whole fresh pineapple, peeled, cored and diced
4 ripe bananas, peeled, sliced and dipped in lemon juice
   to prevent discoloration
2 ripe mangoes, peeled and sliced
fresh lychees (1 can lychees), pitted and halved
disposable aluminum pan
1/4 cup butter (1/2 stick)
1/2 cup brown sugar
1/2 ounce grated fresh ginger
aluminum foil

OPTIONAL

vanilla ice cream or butter pound cake
toasted grated fresh coconut

🍠 Kitchen "prep": Combine fruits in a disposable aluminum pan and drain off all juices. In a sauté pan on low heat, melt butter until it bubbles lightly. Stir in brown sugar and cook until mixture bubbles again. Drain juices from fruits again, then pour sugar mixture over fruits and sprinkle with ginger. Wrap tightly with foil and pack for a picnic.

OUTDOOR COOKING

Place foil-wrapped pan on a hot hibachi and grill until you can smell sugar cooking and caramelizing on fruits; do not burn sugar. Remove foil to monitor cooking. Stir so sugar mixture glazes nicely over fruits.

If desired, spoon fruits over vanilla ice cream or butter pound cake, and top with coconut.

Hibachi Pineapple Spears

Light and refreshing! (Another Patrick Choy creation)

2-pound fresh pineapple, cut in thin spears
   (can substitute fresh mango or guava slices)
aluminum foil
4 tablespoons brown sugar
4 tablespoons butter
freshly ground pepper (optional)

⁚ Lay three or four pineapple spears per person on a piece of foil. Top fruit with a sprinkling of light brown sugar and a small butter dollop. Seal foil packet. Grill on both sides until sugar melts. Open foil and, if desired, top fruits with a little freshly ground pepper.

Mango-Guava Sorbet

Makes 10 (1/2-cup) Servings

Here's a good way to use an overabundance of mangoes. We always have plenty of common mangoes in Kona. People bring them by in the boxes. Some sell, some give.

2 large overripe mangoes, peeled and cut in 1-inch cubes
1 can (6 ounces) frozen guava-nectar concentrate, thawed
sugar to taste

⁚ In a food processor or blender, machine-process all ingredients to form a purée. Freeze for 45 minutes, or until icy.

⁚ Remove mixture from freezer and whip with wire whisk. Refreeze for 45 minutes.

⁚ Remove mixture from freezer and machine-process for 30 seconds. Refreeze until time to serve. Tastes great on a hot summer day.

Desserts

Three-Fruit Sherbet

I freeze the fruit purée until it's like slush. Then whip it with a whisk and refreeze. I like to go through this process three times; it comes out really smooth.

1 ripe medium mango, peeled and seed removed
1-1/2 cans (6 ounces each) passion fruit-nectar concentrate
1 can (13 ounces) pineapple chunks with syrup
1 cup instant nonfat milk powder
1 tablespoon sugar

In a food processor or blender, combine all ingredients and blend well. Pour into a pan and freeze. Great for the hottest times of the summer.

Hilo Haupia Squares

Bake a cookie crust and pour haupia on top of that. It's really, really 'ono (delicious). The macadamia nut cookie crust adds a nice flavor touch.

MACADAMIA COOKIE CRUST

1 cup butter
2 cups flour
1/4 cup light brown sugar
1/2 cup finely chopped macadamia nuts

HAUPIA MIXTURE

2 cans (12 ounces each) frozen coconut milk, thawed
2 cups milk
1 cup sugar
1/2 cup cornstarch
1 cup toasted sweetened flaked coconut
8 ounces chopped fresh Waimea strawberries (optional)

&) Preheat oven to 350°F.

&) In a medium mixing bowl, cut butter into flour with a pastry blender. Stir in brown sugar and macadamia nuts, and mix well. Press dough in a 13 x 9-inch baking pan. Bake 15 minutes or until lightly browned.

&) In a large saucepan, mix coconut milk with milk. Mix sugar with cornstarch, and stir into unheated coconut-milk mixture. Cook on medium heat, stirring frequently, until mixture thickens. Pour mixture over baked crust. Chill. Garnish with coconut and, if desired, strawberries.

COOKING TIP: Oven-toast flaked coconut on a dry baking sheet in a preheated 325°F oven, turning coconut occasionally, until lightly browned.

Easy Banana Pie

This is so easy to make, it's the perfect dessert to serve at a lū'au. Just remember—keep it cool!

1 package (8 ounces) cream cheese, softened
1 cup dairy sour cream
3 tablespoons sugar
3 cups sliced bananas, dipped in lime or lemon juice
Graham Cracker Crust (see recipe below)
whipped cream

৯০ Blend cream cheese and sour cream. Add sugar and mix well. Add bananas.

৯০ Pour into graham cracker crust. Freeze firm. Remove from freezer 5 minutes before serving. Top with whipped cream.

GRAHAM CRACKER CRUST

৯০ Combine 1 cup fine graham cracker crumbs, 2 tablespoons sugar and 3 tablespoons melted butter or margarine. Press firmly (using another pie plate) into unbuttered 9-inch pie plate. Chill until firm, about 45 minutes.

Macadamia Nut Cream Pie

Living in the Kona district on the Big Island gives me great opportunities to create dishes using premium macadamia nuts. I pick the best of the crop and use them in my recipes and restaurants.

In Australia, the home of the macadamia nut, the plant is known as the Queensland nut tree. Introduced to Hawai'i by E.W. Purvis in 1885, this handsome, densely crowned tree matures late, then bears fruit year-round. The nuts are famous for their extremely hard shells and sweet white meats.

3 egg yolks
3 cups milk
3/4 cup granulated sugar
1/3 cup cornstarch
1/4 teaspoon salt
2 tablespoons butter
1-1/2 teaspoons vanilla extract
1 cup roasted and chopped macadamia nuts
1 9-inch baked pie shell

✇ Combine egg yolks, milk, sugar, cornstarch, salt, and butter. Bring to a boil over medium heat, stirring constantly. Boil for 1 minute, and remove from heat. Stir in vanilla and macadamia nuts. Pour into pie shell, and chill covered with plastic wrap.

Banana Poi—Tahitian-Style
with Haupia Ice Cream

This isn't two-finger poi. It is fork poi, baked from bananas. Topped with haupia ice cream and sugar-dusted won ton chips and swirls of coconut syrup, it's really 'onolicious.

6 ripe bananas
2 tablespoons granulated sugar
1/4 cup lemon juice
1/2 cup water
2 tablespoons cornstarch
1 tablespoon vanilla
1/2 cup water
vegetable oil spray
4 scoops haupia (coconut) ice cream
1/2 cup coconut syrup
1 cup won ton chips dusted with powdered sugar

GARNISH

4 mint leaf sprigs

🔊 Preheat oven to 350°F.

🔊 In a medium saucepan, mash bananas, then add sugar, lemon juice and water. Simmer for 30 minutes. Pour banana mixture into a blender, or use a hand blender to purée.

🔊 In a small bowl, mix water and cornstarch together. Add vanilla and cornstarch mixture to banana purée and blend well.

🔊 Grease an 8 x 8-inch baking pan with vegetable oil spray. Pour banana mixture into baking pan and cover baking pan with aluminum foil. Bake for 30 to 45 minutes. Halfway through the baking process remove the aluminum foil. Remove from oven and cool for 4 to 5 hours in the refrigerator.

🔊 Cut baked banana poi into four pieces and place into individual large bowls. Serve with haupia ice cream. Drizzle with coconut syrup and sprinkle with won ton chips dusted with powdered sugar. Garnish with mint leaves.

Pineapple Coconut Yum Yum

This dessert is aptly named—people will love this tropical treat.

BOTTOM CRUST

1 cup butter
2/3 cup sugar
1/2 teaspoon vanilla
1-1/2 cups flour
1 cup chopped macadamia nuts

FILLING

1 cup sugar
1 tablespoon cornstarch
1 can (No. 2) crushed pineapple with juice
1/2 cup shredded coconut

TOPPING

1/2 cup sugar
1/2 cup butter
1/4 cup flour
2 cups oatmeal

To make bottom crust, cream butter and sugar. Add vanilla, flour and nuts. Press into the bottom of a 9 by 13-inch pan and bake for 10 minutes in a preheated 350°F oven.

To make the filling, combine sugar and cornstarch in a small saucepan. Add the crushed pineapple and pineapple juice. Cook over medium heat until thickened. Add the coconut and pour over crust.

For the topping, cream the sugar and butter. Mix in the flour. Add oatmeal and blend well. Cut dough into the size of peas and sprinkle evenly over the filling. Pat down firmly. Bake at 350°F for about 35 minutes, or until lightly browned.

Drinks

The number one drink for a lūʻau? Water! All that outdoor cooking, serving and eating creates a big thirst. Be sure you have plenty of cold water in bottles or an easily accessible faucet and an ice bucket. Then you can think about the other types of beverages you want to serve.

A big container of island fruit punch is always great for the kids. For a "kid-kick," dip the rim of their punch cup in li hing powder! Soda and beer are easy in a cooler. If you are serving two kinds of lūʻau punch, "with" and "without," they should be clearly marked with an adult assigned to the serving.

If your lūʻau includes a bar, the tropical drink choices are endless. Make them in pink, blue and pineapple varieties and don't forget the paper umbrella and the orchid on the side! Many can be made without alcohol. Outside the glasses should always be plastic. Remember, the best, last drink of the party is always a big mug of Kona coffee.

Tropical Fruit Punch

Makes 4 Servings

1 tablespoon li hing mui powder
1 cup of ice cubes
1 orange, peeled and cut into segments
1 cup sliced fresh papaya
2 strawberries
1 cup diced mango
1 small banana
1 cup fresh fruit juice (such as orange juice)
8 blueberries
8 raspberries
1 cup diced pineapple

🍃 Purée all ingredients together in a blender, except the blueberries, raspberries, and pineapple. Blend till smooth. Fold in the remaining fruit and pour into chilled glasses. Enjoy on a nice summer day!

Haupia with a Kick, "Oh Yeah"

Makes 1 Serving

1 ounce light rum
2 ounces Coco Lopez coconut syrup
1 ounce half & half cream
ice

GARNISH

1 orchid

🍃 Fill blender with ice to 1/3 full. Blend all ingredients, then pour into a Viva Grande glass, and garnish with an orchid.

Sam's North Shore Smoothie

1 ounce vodka
1 ounce orange juice
1 ounce cranberry juice
2 ounces strawberry purée
1 ounce grenadine syrup
ice

GARNISH

3 tablespoons whipped cream
1 maraschino cherry

& Omega; Fill blender with ice to 1/3 full. Add ingredients, and blend. Pour mixture into a Viva Grande glass, and top with whipped cream. Garnish with a maraschino cherry.

Lava Flow— Get It While It's Hot!!!

Makes 1 Serving

2 ounces strawberry purée
1 ounce light rum
1 ounce pineapple juice
1 ounce sweet & sour juice
1 ounce coconut syrup
1 ounce half & half cream
ice

GARNISH

1/4 slice of pineapple
1 orchid

Ω Pour strawberry purée into a 14-ounce hurricane glass. Fill blender with ice to 1/3 full, and add all other ingredients. Purée until slushy. Tilt hurricane glass to the side, and gently pour blender purée down the inside of the glass, careful not to disturb the strawberry purée.

Scorpion in a Glass

1 ounce light rum
1 ounce brandy
2 ounces orange juice
1 ounce orgeat syrup
ice

GARNISH

1/4 slice of orange

🐚 Fill blender with ice to a little less than 1/4 full. Add ingredients, and blend. Pour mixture into a champagne flute, and garnish with 1/4 slice of orange.

Guava Colada from the Valley

Makes 1 Serving

1 ounce light rum
1 ounce pineapple juice
2 ounces guava juice (concentrate)
1 ounce Coco Lopez coconut syrup
1 ounce half & half cream
ice

GARNISH

1/4 of a pineapple slice
1 orchid

🐚 Fill blender with ice to 1/3 full. Add ingredients, and blend until slushy. Pour into a hurricane glass, and garnish with 1/4 of a pineapple slice and an orchid.

Kona Mac Freeze

1 ounce Kahlua
1 ounce Kahana Mac Nut Liqueur
1 ounce half & half cream
ice

GARNISH

3 tablespoons whipped cream
1 teaspoon ground macadamia nuts

🔊 Fill blender with ice to 1/3 full. Add ingredients, and blend until creamy. Pour into a Viva Grande glass to 1/4 inch from the top. Add whipped cream, and sprinkle with ground macadamia nuts.

Loco Loco Mocha Mocha

Makes 1 Serving

1 ounce Coco Rum
1 ounce Kahlua
1 ounce half & half
3 ounces pineapple juice
1 ounce Kahuluacino
ice

GARNISH

3 tablespoons whipped cream
cocoa powder (for dusting)
1 maraschino cherry

🔊 Squirt chocolate syrup around the inside of a 14-ounce hurricane glass. Fill blender with ice to 1/3 full. Add ingredients, and blend until creamy. Pour into the hurricane glass, leaving 1/4 inch at the top. Cap with whipped cream, and a dash of cocoa dust. Place cherry on whipped cream.

Over the Rainbow

Makes 1 Serving ·

1 ounce Malibu rum
2 ounces pineapple juice
2 ounces cranberry juice
1 ounce Midori liqueur
ice

GARNISH

1/4 slice of pineapple
1 orchid

  Fill a hurricane glass with ice. Add ingredients. Float with 1 ounce of Midori liqueur, and garnish with 1/4 slice of pineapple and an orchid.

Tropical Crab Itch

Makes 1 Serving

1 ounce orange curacao
2 ounces orange juice
1 ounce orgeat syrup
1 ounce dark rum
ice

GARNISH

1/4 slice of pineapple
1 orchid
1 back scratcher (optional)

  Fill blender with ice to 1/3 full. Add orange curacao, orange juice, and orgeat syrup. Blend until slushy, and pour into a hurricane glass. Float with dark rum, and garnish with 1/4 slice of pineapple, an orchid and a back scratcher!

INDEX

Other Sam Choy Books
by Mutual Publishing:

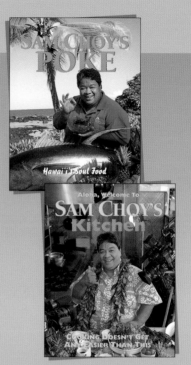

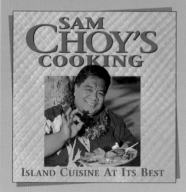

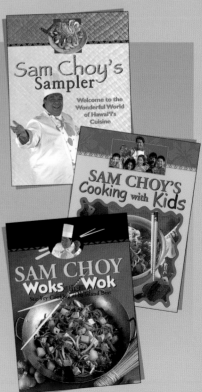

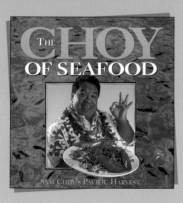

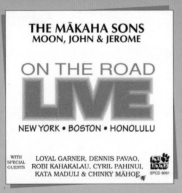